"Jean is a unique and important voice in the large law, librarian, and l̲e̲g̲a̲l̲ and innovation communities. There are not many journalists who care about legal technology so much that they write about it, raise challenging questions and, perhaps more significantly, do the hard work necessary to keep themselves fluent in emerging technologies. I believe that these voices are critically important to the legal community overall.

Jean brings a unique perspective. She's an experienced end user, but also someone who is a careful follower of legal trends, and issues affecting law firm reputation, budget and business success. Her blog is an invaluable resource to anyone interested in the same.

—Charlotte Rushton
Managing Director, US Law Firms

"Jean O'Grady is one of the foremost legal market visionaries. Her insight on knowledge management, law libraries, and legal research is unparalleled. I always look forward to reading her blog posts – I learn a lot from them."

—Ron Friedmann, Partner, Fireman & Company
Blogger at Strategic Legal Technology Blog

"Dewey B Strategic is a must-read resource. If you want to understand the fast-moving world of legal information, you need to start right here."

—Ed Walters, CEO, Fastcase

"Jean and her widely-loved Dewey B Strategic blog have provided invaluable support to so many of us looking to bring new technology into the profession. It is one of the few places I check every day to stay abreast of the legal tech field."

—Pablo Arredondo
Co-Founder and Chief Legal Research Officer, Casetext

"I check Dewey B Strategic every morning. The blog is a must-read for anyone who needs to understand critical developments in legal innovation, technology, and knowledge management. The site's continuing influence and relevance is a testament to its author, Jean O'Grady, whose unique insight and extensive knowledge are unparalleled in the legal profession."

—Dean Sonderegger, VP Legal Markets & Innovation
Wolters Kluwer, Legal and Regulatory U.S.

"Jean O'Grady's insights into the landscape and future of legal tech and legal information have been spot-on, making her Dewey B Strategic blog a must-read for the industry. She is an optimistic, reliable, and realistic knowledge strategist who makes all the connections between big ideas and specific practice.

–Lucy Curci-Gonzalez, Executive Director
New York Law Institute

"Dewey B Strategic is a must read blog for knowledge management and informational professionals who want to be in the know about the latest technology tools relevant to legal practice and trends shaping the changing legal landscape.

–Steve Lastres
Dir. of Research and Knowledge Management Services
Debevoise & Plimpton

"I rely upon Dewey B Strategic to help me stay informed about the legal community in general, and our profession in particular. Jean is a great forecaster. Her sharp insights are delivered with humor, and with an eye on the future we can claim for ourselves if we will."

–Keith Ann Stiverson
Director of the Library/Senior Lecturer
IIT Chicago-Kent College of Law

"You can't be in legal tech without understanding the importance of Dewey B Strategic. As a thought leader and avid tech reviewer, Jean's words are heard in the board rooms of every legaltech company because they have such influence in law firms across the county."

–Josh Becker, CEO, Lex Machina

"Jean O'Grady, author of Dewey B Strategic, has been an important and influential voice within the world of law for many years. She both tracks and influences the evolving legal publishing and tech environment, and her opinion plays a major role in these spaces."

–David Lat, Founder, Above the Law
Author of Supreme Ambitions

"Jean O'Grady is a pioneer in citizen journalism in every sense of the word. Her blog, *Dewey B Strategic* is recognized across the legal profession for its keen insight and commentary on legal innovation, legal services products, information management and more. When O'Grady talks, people in legal listen.

–Kevin O'Keefe, CEO & Founder, Lexblog

Dewey B Strategic

Risk, value, strategy, innovation,

knowledge and the legal profession.

2017 Blog-o-zine

JEAN P. O'GRADY

Year of the Book
135 Glen Avenue
Glen Rock, PA 17327

ISBN 13: 978-1-945670-85-5
ISBN 10: 1-945670-85-1

Library of Congress Control Number: 2018933943

Table of Contents

2017

Introduction

Dear Colleagues and Readers:

You must be asking yourselves, "Why a print blog-o-zine?" Why would I, who have been an unrelenting advocate for digital information consumption, now pivot to embrace a print representation of my blog posts? The bottom line is that I want to make my content accessible to more readers and to make is more easily "browse-able" for lawyers, researchers, and legal information innovators who want to review a recent snapshot of the legal information landscape.

I had two epiphanies on the print versus digital issue in 2017. After seven years of blogging it has become more difficult for me to locate my prior blogs. After I moved from the Blogger platform to Lexblog which uses WordPress, my earlier posts became increasingly hard to find using Google searches. As I often say, "Google can always give you something, but it does not always give you the exact thing you are looking for."

Perhaps more importantly, in 2017 I read the book *The Revenge of Analog: Real Things and Why They Matter*, by David Sax, which posits that since we are material beings we have a special connection to tangible things. The book documents the reappearance of all sorts of artifacts of our pre-digital age: phonograph players, vinyl records, 35mm film, moleskin notebooks and yes – specialist magazines! I was only halfway through the book when my daughter asked to go into an Urban Outfitters on 5th Avenue at 42nd Street in Manhattan – and what was in the front of the store? Displays of phonograph players, vinyl records and 35mm Fuji film.

The Revenge of Analog made me question one of my most basic assumptions about information delivery. It made me notice that for at least some content, I prefer to hold something in my hands and browse.

The *2017 Dewey B Strategic Blog-o-zine* is intended to be an easy access, reference handbook on the major legal research and technology trends, product releases and enhancements of 2017.

2017: KM Rises Again. "Robot Lawyer" Fatigue Sets In. Analytics and Workflow Surge.

Knowledge Management Comes of Age. 2017 was the year that *The American Lawyer* finally changed the name of their annual library survey to the "Survey of Library, Knowledge Management and Research." The accompanying articles acknowledge the rise of Chief Knowledge Officers in law firms. In 2016 I chided ALM for having reported the death or print law libraries since 2002 – the same headline spanning fourteen years. It was time to move on and acknowledge that information professionals are leading a wide variety of knowledge management initiatives involving not only internal documents, but marrying external analytics to internal business intelligence and pushing competitive insights into lawyer workflow. I started my first KM project in 1986 when the outputs were referred to as work product and brief banks. KM then became a "dirty word" associated with the "trough of disillusionment" in the "hype cycle." I have a theory that during the intervening 30 years KM fell into disfavor. By the early 2000s KM initiatives were shunted into IT Departments. KM projects were reduced to software deployments often led by smart IT guys who had no first hand understanding of legal documents, legal taxonomy, or legal research. Library and information professionals have gotten a second shot at influencing the development of the next generation of KM tools in a world where clients demand both efficiency and custom insights arising from the blending of internal and external content. The next generation of KM will involve AI, and human experts will be training machines.

It's Not AI, It's Just Software! At long last, the relentless and cringe worthy "robot lawyer" headlines were greeted with the groans and eyeball rolling they deserve. At the 2017 ARK KM conference in New York, "artificial intelligence" was publicly rebuked by several speakers as hype. One panelist pointed out that all the software created since Babbage's "difference engine" have offered artificial intelligence. At the AALL Conference in July, Professor Susan Nevelow-Mart, of the University of Colorado Law School called out Ross's Andrew Arruda for the secrecy surrounding his product's "black box" marketing.

AI vs Analytics. AI offers buzz-worthy sound bites, but in my humble opinion, in 2017 analytics products were a better investment than most off the shelf AI products. Longer term, a combination of AI and analytics will be a powerful game changer. In 2017 analytics offered more immediate impact in the law firms by providing easily accessible, custom insights and data to support AFAs, pitch metrics and litigation strategy.

Analytics products continue to expand. Lex Machina added Bankruptcy Appeals, Commercial, Product Liability, Employment and new "apps" for litigation damages and parties. Ravel Law offered law firm rankings and Bloomberg Law added judge's analytics. Thomson Reuters although first to offer an analytics product for marketers and researchers did not add analytics to Westlaw in 2017. Fingers crossed – we will see something in 2018.

I See Predictive Tools in Our Future. Lexis and Wolters Kluwer are offering predictive legislation. Manzama rolled out its predictive dashboard for monitoring industry and company health as indicators of business opportunity.

Key Developments in Legal Products – The Start Ups

- *Fastcase* grows up and hired a seasoned legal publishing executive, Steve Errick, and launches a print publishing imprint: Full Court Press.
- *Casetext* enters the "push" market with the launch of Brief Finder which delivers newly filed briefs to attorneys.
- *Gavelytics* and *Judicata* "Green shoots" of state analytics, for California. Gavelytics offers county court analytics and Judicata offers a complete "grading" of briefs based on historic California appellate analytics.
- *Ravel* launches law firm analytics and rankings.
- *Voxgov,* although marketing to academic law libraries for a while, in 2017 they discovered the law firm market. Voxgov offers a massive collection of government releases, reports, as well as granular analytics on government activities and trends.

The Saddest Development was the acquisition of Ravel Law by LexisNexis. I always admired Ravel's founders for having identified judicial insights that had been ignored by CALR pioneers Lexis and Westlaw for decades. Using algorithms and analytics, Ravel had targeted and uncovered the specific language in specific precedents which judges cite when they are deciding an issue. It was always there in the opinions! My hat is off to Daniel Lewis and Nik Reed for their breakthrough insights. I am happy to report that so far, LexisNexis seems to be allowing Ravel to continue as a sort of independent "skunkworks" for innovation while also migrating Ravel insights and content into several different LexisNexis platforms.

Key Developments: The Big 4 Legal Publishers

Bad Data. "Fake news" was in the air and real mistakes were found in legal products. Lexis was sued for errors in one of their "color books." Thomson Reuters disclosed some errors in their Monitor Suite Analytics.

Lexis Continues Acquiring and Begins to Integrate. I have been begging LexisNexis to integrate the content from their multiple acquisitions. While Lexis is not rebuilding an integrated mix of products from the ground up, they are continuing to find ways to integrate new content. In 2016 they made selected Lex Machina data available on Lexis Advance. In 2017 they integrated Intelligize features into Lexis Practice Advisor. Lexis launched a streaming video federal practice guide from Wagstaffe. On the AI front, Lexis rolled out "Lexis Answers" to fast track lawyers to quick answers to federal and state questions.

Wolters Kluwer Launches Innovation Year-Round. Even I was surprised by Wolters Kluwer's stunning string of launches. Dean Sonderegger, VP of Legal Markets and Innovation, has made no secret of WK's agile approach to product development and it appears to have paid off in 2017. They partnered with KM Standards, a machine learning company, to launch M&A Clause Analytics and entered into an alliance with intellectual property analytics company ktMINE to enhance Wolters Kluwer's IP offerings. They also launched a cybersecurity product, enhanced their unique international arbitration platform, added predictive legislation to the Federal Knowledge Center, and developed "Smart tasks" for corporate know-how drafting.

Bloomberg Law: New Features and New Content. They launched a Data Compliance Risk benchmarking tool, added judge's analytics, docket key for searching within dockets, e-discovery practice center, new practice portfolios, added AI enabled research features: "points of law" and "citation maps," and relaunched their Corporate Practice Center.

Thomson Reuters: The Big Silence One of the big surprises of 2017 was Thomson Reuters' silence. They continue watching their competitors release analytics for lawyers and products featuring machine learning and artificial intelligence. They announced a partnership with Watson over a year ago yet maintained the silence of a Sphinx. The only product announcement I covered in 2017 was the relaunch of their online treatise platform. No doubt there will be a *huge* announcement in 2018.

Bonus Content Free and Great:

The Best Laugh: Columbia Law Revue's Music Video Parody of Lexis, Westlaw and Bloomberg Law. https://youtu.be/7SmA22EosTY

The Best New Newsletter. AALL began producing a wonderful daily newsletter "Know it AALL: Your Daily Connection to the News You Need." Wonderful compilation of legal information and technology news aggregated from a wide variety of sources. It never disappoints... And it's free!

Jean O'Grady
February 1, 2018
Washington, D.C.

2017 Trends in Law Firms and Legal Publishing: Pure Speculation from the Serious to the Fantastic

JANUARY 9, 2017

A few ideas on what we might or might not see develop in 2017:

Thomson Reuters Predictive. 2017 has to be the year when Thomson Reuters launches a predictive product for lawyers. Early in 2016 the organization rebranded itself as "The Answer Company." They entered into a relationship with IBM to gain access to IBM's Watson artificial intelligence technology. Several months ago TR announced a predictive legal product for financial analysts. TR Legal has remained silent as their competitors – both large (Lexis/Lex Machina, Bloomberg BNA) and small (Ravel, Ross, CARA, LitIQ) – launched a variety of headline grabbing predictive and AI research products. TR has been quietly investing in their Innovation Labs. TR owns all the same data which is driving their competitors' predictive and AI products... so what are they waiting for? It has to be a predictive product that goes a step beyond their competitors... or they would have already launched it. Perhaps a product that combines transactional and litigation data? Perhaps a product that integrates predictive data into a workflow/drafting tool? I can't wait to see what it is. I expect TR to be hosting an especially interesting launch party at the AALL conference in July. I hope I am not disappointed.

LexisNexis Will Not Purchase Any New Products in 2017. They will spend the year integrating all the premium resources they have bought over the past five years (Lex Machina, Newsdesk, MLex, Law360, Knowledge Mosaic, Intelligize) into a single game-changing integrated platform. Okay, I don't think this is actually going to happen – just putting it out there in case LexisNexis' CEO Mike Walsh is reading my blog today. I seriously think it is time to stop collecting the crown jewels of the legal market and start building some synergies between these resources.

Bloomberg BNA will Purchase Wolters Kluwer or Wolters Kluwer will Purchase Bloomberg BNA. It has been rumored that Mike Bloomberg planned to give Bloomberg Law 100 years to beat out Thomson Reuters and LexisNexis to become the dominant legal information product in the U.S. Bloomberg Law has been on the market for less than a decade and has faced some serious headwinds. By now, Mr. Bloomberg has certainly begun to notice that it is a lot easier to get an investment bank to sign on to a multi-million dollar subscription than it is to slide a million dollar product into a law firm budget. The zero-based budget still reigns in most law firms, so these two legal publishing giants, Wolters Kluwer and Bloomberg BNA, could benefit from combining their product lines. Both publishers have been dominant players, offering regulatory expertise, and could gain additional market share in a legal market competing to anticipate and track the regulatory uncertainties arising from the incoming Presidential administration.

The Trump Deregulation Watch. Shortly after I moved to Washington, D.C., at the start of the Clinton administration in 1993, President Bill Clinton launched the Reinvent Government Initiative which was supposed to dramatically streamline regulation and shrink the Federal Register and the Code of Federal Regulations (CFR) – the official source of all U.S. regulations. I recalled front page photos of President Clinton and Vice President Al Gore posing with pallets of the regulatory materials they planned to eliminate.

Figure 1: Reinvent Government 1993 Style

Will the CFR actually shrink over the next four years? Let's look at history... in 1993 the CFR was a 200-volume set. In 2016 there were 248 volumes. So the long-term outcome of the earlier "Reinvent government initiative" has resulted in a 25% increase in the volume of regulations over the past 23 years.

Law Librarians Will Put an End to Fake News by Creating a "Uniform System of Web Citation." Just as judges toss briefs which fail to cite authorities for all legal propositions, it is time to require "news" websites to include cite-able authorities. Law librarians should collaborate on a new publication which I propose to be called *The Uniform System of Web Citation*. This publication will include 400 pages of rules following the example of the "Blue Book" Editors. The "Blue Book" rule 18.2.1 on citing Internet sources provides an excellent inspiration point:

18.2.1 General Internet Citation Principles (p. 180)

(a) Sources that can be cited as if to the original print source.

When an authenticated, official, or exact copy of a source is available online, citation can be made as if to the original print source (without any URL information appended). Many states have begun to discontinue printed official legal resources, instead relying on online versions as the official resources for administrative or legislative documents. The federal government is also moving toward increasing access to online versions of legal documents, though it continues to publish official print versions.

(i) Authenticated documents.

When citing to such materials, *The Bluebook* encourages citation to "authenticated" sources: those that use an encryption-based authentication method, such as a digital signature or public key infrastructure, to ensure the accuracy of the online source. Generally, an authenticated document will have a certificate or logo indicating that a government entity verified that the document is complete and unaltered.

If all fake news authors were required to read "blue book" style rules before posting any "news" – sheer boredom and mental fatigue alone would dramatically reduce the volume of nonsense posted to the web.

(Lest anyone mistake this blog post for real news – let me be clear – this is a suggestion – not a fact.)

Figure 2: Pop Up Law Firms Emerge in DC – It will be HUGE!

Pop Up Law Firms in D.C. Remember the Occupy Wall Street Camps which sprung up in parks around D.C. in 2011? I wouldn't be surprised if 2017 brings "pop up" law firms to D.C. Law firms without D.C. satellite offices know that something "huge" is about to happen there and they want to be part of the action. In a nod to ongoing client demands for efficiency, smart law firms will gain a D.C. presence without having to spring for an $80 per square foot lease by establishing a "pop up" presence on the National Mall.

Every Law Firm Will Have a Robot Lawyer. But the robot will not be practicing law. This new breed of robot will drive lawyer efficiency by having one function — dealing with passwords. They will troubleshoot all password problems and be the repository for all 1,000+ passwords which the average lawyer manages in order to access everything from the law firm network, to their daily news subscriptions, CLE training, health care accounts, voicemail, meal accounts, travel reimbursement accounts, the spam blocker account, the time and billing account, client extranets, and the 500 specialized research platforms each lawyer needs to practice law.

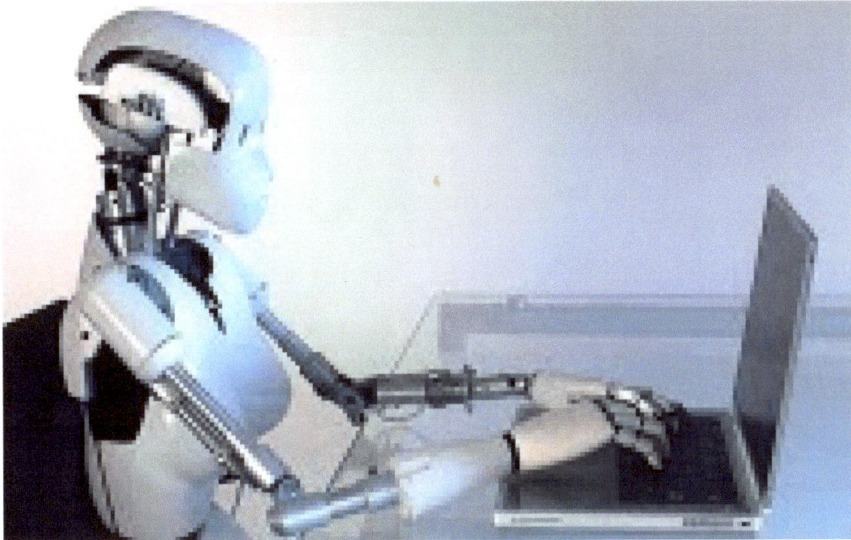

Password robots will reduce time wasted on lost passwords, password resetting, trying to remember the password you made up two minutes ago because it conformed to the 16 arbitrary criteria required for reset and has no mnemonic qualities, mandatory password strengthening exercises, clearing caches of old passwords, synching mobile and network device passwords, and replacing laptops which have been flung across the office in frustration at the appearance of a random "your password has expired message." Password robots are expected to boost lawyer productivity by recovering 10 to 20 hours of wasted time per month which translates into an estimated $100,000 increase in annual billable time per lawyer.

And if none of this happens… there is always next year.

Trump Deregulation Watch: Wolters Kluwer Publishers White Paper, Bloomberg BNA Publishes 2017 Outlook Reports

JANUARY 11, 2017

Wolters Kluwer
Law & Business

Wolters Kluwer and Bloomberg BNA's editorial teams have built their editorial credibility on comprehensive and exacting tracking of U.S. regulatory changes. The incoming Trump administration appears to be poised to shake up the established regulatory framework through both deregulation and statutory repeal. I reached out to executives at Wolters Kluwer and Bloomberg BNA to find out how they are preparing for the Trump Deregulation Agenda. Although both publishers suggest that preparation for this transition of government is "business as usual," both have also issued special reports. In addition, Wolters Kluwer is planning some major editorial enhancements to existing products which will make tracking regulatory changes easier.

Dean Sonderegger, Wolters Kluwer's VP & GM of Legal Markets & Innovation, provided a statement from the WK editorial team:

> Wolters Kluwer is poised to cover the legislative and regulatory impact of the incoming Trump Administration with the same level of timely, comprehensive, and objective analysis that has been our mainstay for decades. Ted Trautmann, Editor-in-Chief, states: "Nothing will change in our approach. What is different, however, is the magnitude of the new agenda — from repeal of Obamacare and Dodd-Frank, to massive reform of current tax, immigration, energy, and trade policy, to the rollback of signature rulemaking initiatives of the Labor Department, EPA, and other agencies, as well as many Obama Administration executive orders." These potential changes, explained in a recent Wolters Kluwer white paper, are so sweeping as to warrant heightened vigilance to help our customers plan

and prepare. Whatever awaits, the Wolters Kluwer team of experts is ready to help organizations navigate the changing regulatory landscape.

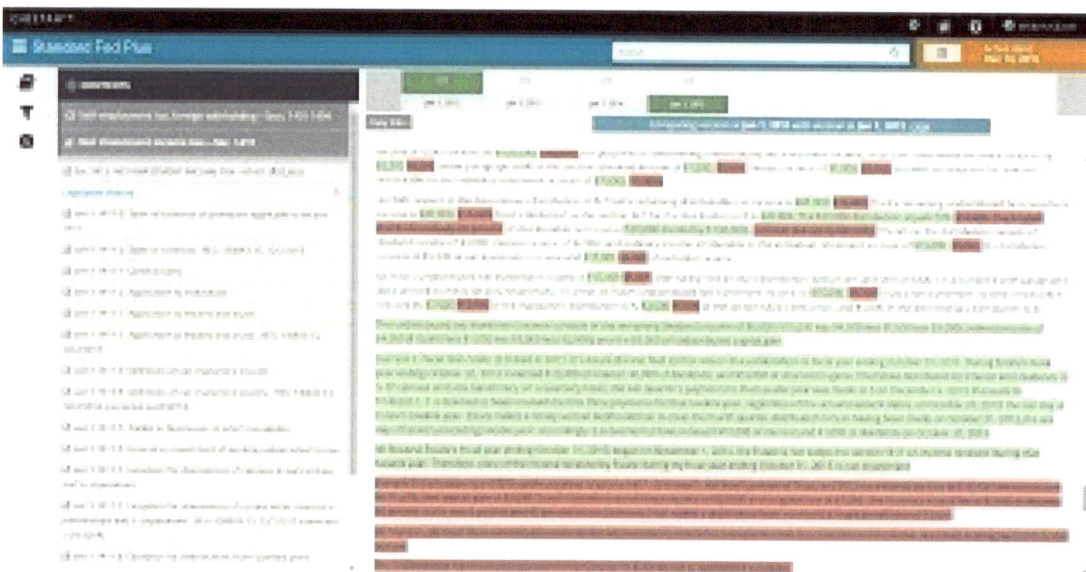

Figure 3: Wolters Kluwer Regulation Redliner

Right now Wolters Kluwer is not planning any new products to address the change in administration. Their statement underscored "our ongoing commitment to diligently track changes and update our customers as quickly as as possible:

> *...we do believe it's important to address the workflow that attorneys and researchers utilize when dealing with legislative changes. To that end, we are enhancing our products that track regulatory events to enable researchers to quickly determine changes to laws, regulations, and guidance and comparing those changes to particular points-in-time in the past.*

In January, Wolters Kluwer will release an enhancement to the Standard *Federal Tax Reporter* which they are calling *"Standard Fed Plus."*

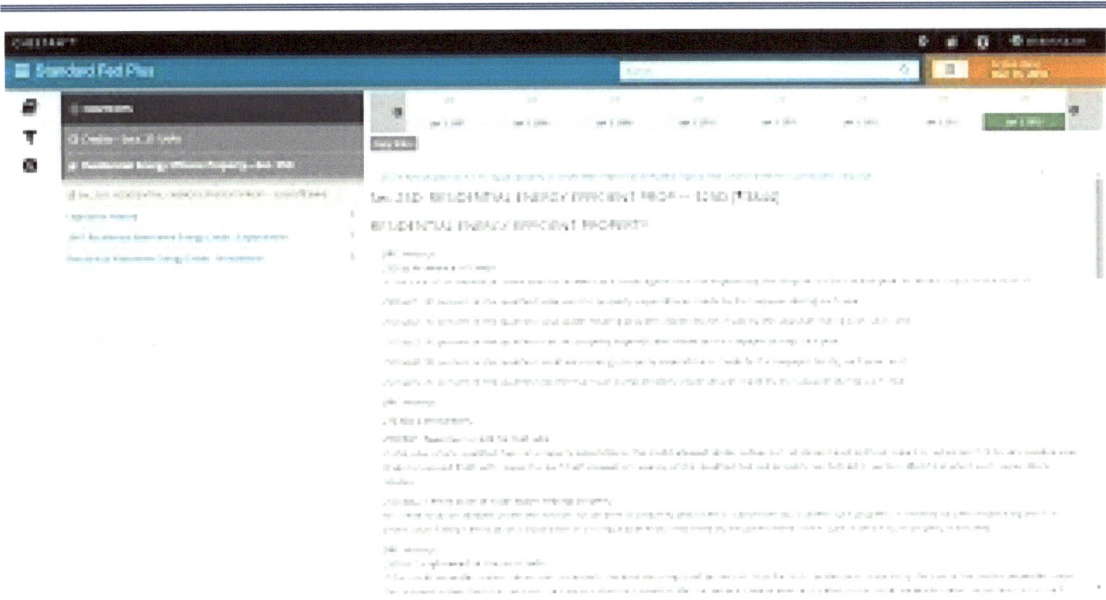

Figure 4: WK Standard Fed Plus -" Point in Time" Changes

Here is a description of the product from the upcoming press release:

"*Standard Fed Plus* is a first-to-market, centralized, online product that helps tax professionals understand U.S. federal tax law changes. *Standard Fed Plus* provides point-in-time analysis that enables legal professionals to see legal tax changes in context, with redlining capability to visually show where changes have occurred at a point-in-time or to compare differences in the laws, regulations, guidance or commentary between points-in-time. It also includes a calendar feature to help attorneys more accurately and quickly research changes in the tax law back to 1986 and on a weekly basis going forward. The exclusive redlining feature of the *Standard Fed Plus* provides tax attorneys with a solution that increases the accuracy, efficiency, and speed of legal tax research to enable them to more quickly understand legal tax changes and provide more accurate tax advice to clients."

**Bloomberg
BNA**

The Bloomberg BNA Approach: Outlook Reports

I also asked Bloomberg BNA's new President Scott Mozarsky if Bloomberg BNA was making any special preparations for the Trump Administration. According to him, "Bloomberg BNA's D.C.-based bureau of reporters and editors will closely track Trump administration regulatory and enforcement changes in all the key federal agencies. In fact, before the election we were reporting on what a Trump administration might do moving forward."

Bloomberg Law subscribers will be able to get an early preview of Trump's agenda in a series of Outlook 2017 special reports, including agencies regulating financial services, labor and employment, international trade, privacy, healthcare, environment, the tech sector, and telecommunications. Additionally, live events have been planned around several topics that will feature Bloomberg BNA experts and thought leaders (see Bloomberg BNA's Outlook 2017 website for more information: https://www.bna.com/2017-Outlook/).

Here is the list of Outlook reports currently posted on Bloomberg's Website.

- Intellectual Property, Privacy, Tech & Telecom
- Tax & Accounting
- Financial Services
- International Employment Law
- International Trade
- International Payroll
- Health Care
- Environment & Energy
- Labor & Employment
- U.S. Payroll (January 25, 2017)

For other topics, in addition to news coverage, Bloomberg Law offers specialized regulatory alerts to monitor agency activities. Mozarsky noted that the anticipated changes to the Affordable Care Act will be tracked in Bloomberg Law's Federal Health Care Regulatory Alert, and environmental agencies can be closely tracked with the EHS Federal Regulatory Alert.

Bloomberg BNA is also releasing several regulatory trackers following federal and state regulatory activity related to emerging technologies. Bloomberg Law subscribers have access to these unique resources that cross jurisdictions and agencies for technologies that will reshape industries. Examples include autonomous vehicles and fintech.

Voxgov: A Veritable Goldmine of "Hidden" U.S. Government Insights and Trends

JANUARY 19, 2017

"Uncertainty" is the word which best describes the atmosphere in Washington, D.C., as the city prepares for the new administration. This uncertainty is driving traffic to a relatively new product called voxgov. The voxgov website offers a treasure-trove of hidden government data and an alerting system for anyone trying to understand the statements and positions of government agencies and officials related to any issue. At last count, voxgov contained over 26 million government documents.

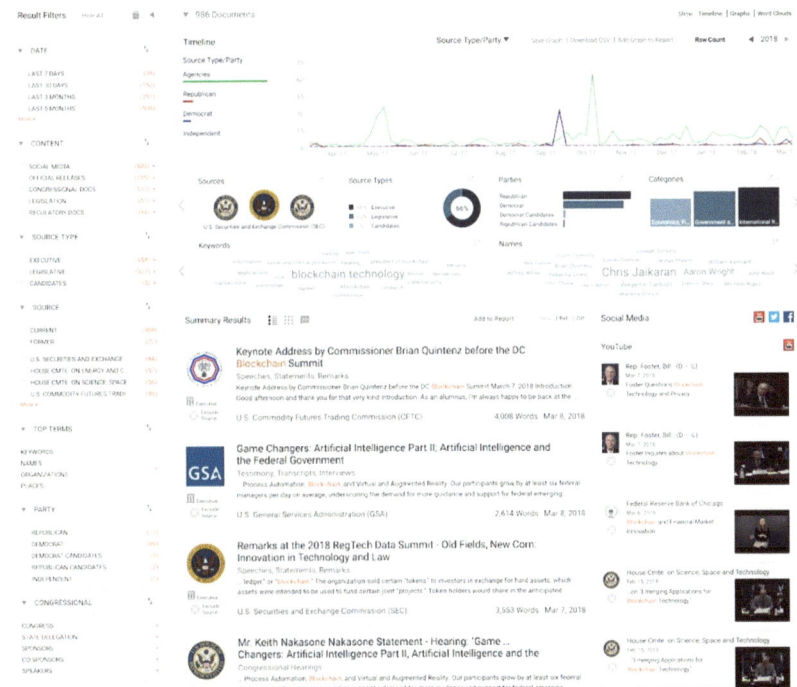

Figure 5: voxgov "Hacking" trends

The government information that lawyers normally rely upon, such as statutes and regulations, only represents about 10% of the voxgov database. The vast majority of government materials in voxgov are collected from over 14,000 government websites. The document types include: Press Releases, News, Notices, Columns, Articles, Op-Eds, Decisions, Opinions, Orders, Events, Media Advisories, Fact Sheets, Newsletters, Bulletins, Recalls, Alerts, Reports, Publications, Speeches, Statements, Remarks, Testimony, and Transcripts, along with Social Media from official government sources, Twitter, Facebook, YouTube and more. voxgov only collects information authored or adopted by the U.S. Federal Government and published on official government websites. All of the data is enriched with extensive metadata which supports sophisticated filtering and trending.

voxgov is the brainchild of an Australian attorney Robert Dessau. After passing the New York State bar, Dessau built a successful consulting business working with Australian technology companies seeking U.S. market entry. During this time he recognized the difficulty of accessing valuable information generated by agencies of the U.S. Government. Based on this overwhelming need, Dessau has been dedicated to building and developing the back-end systems and know-how for the voxgov platform that exists today.

Dessau moved from collecting documents to analyzing trends and parsing the people, agencies, parties, and issues stirring the pot of government advocacy and regulation. He built a system for indexing and analyzing the reports and data produced by over 9,000 U.S. Government sources. Today voxgov also includes over 24 million social media posts. Even though the U.S. Government has migrated much of their standard legislative and regulatory materials online, the vast majority of government information remains hidden even though available in digital format.

No, You Can't Google This Stuff. Years ago I heard Ralph Nader remark that U.S. Government reports were a goldmine of data that no one wanted to read. Their plain brown covers and austere typeface screamed "boring." Those were the bad old days before the digital revolution, and for those of you who thought all government data was just a Google search away from your eyeballs... voxgov will show you just how wrong you are. According to Dessau, less than 1% of all government documents are available on the web. voxgov's proprietary technology visits over 14,600 U.S. Government web destinations on algorithmically generated intervals of time, in search of new documents published to any of these source sites.

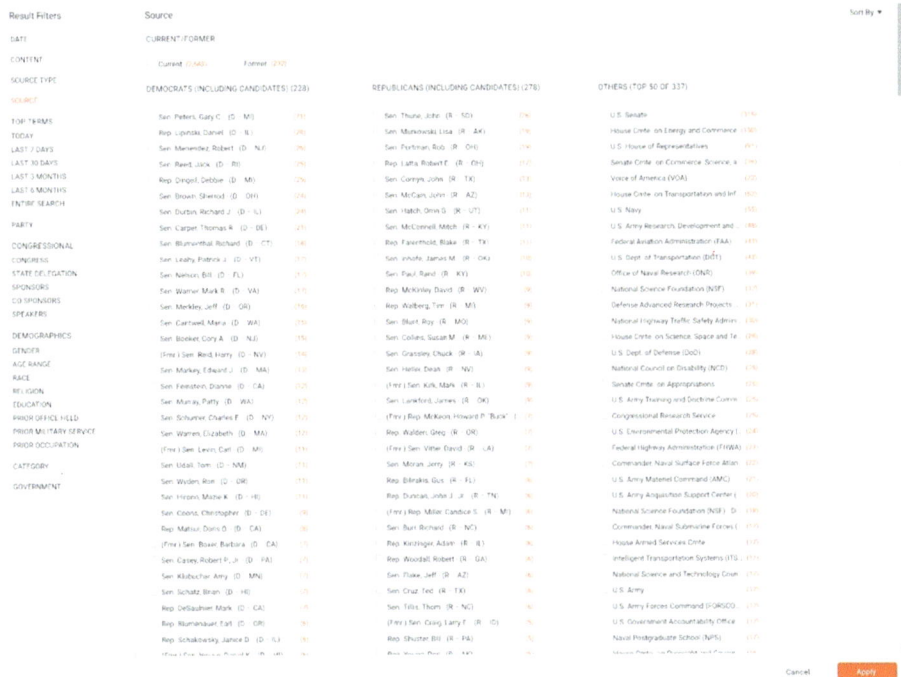

Figure 6: Cybersecurity-related terms, people, agencies

The Trump Effect. In recent weeks voxgov's phones have been ringing "off the hook." The voxgov team has fielded requests from a wide variety of stakeholders needing to glean insights into the new administration. Inquiries include: A city facing a budget crisis if federal funding to Sanctuary Cities is withdrawn; a bank reading contradictory indicators on economic policy under the next administration; a pharmaceutical group preparing to navigate a new legislative and regulatory environment. According to Dessau, people are turning to voxgov to address a common need "for the ability to telescope into who is saying what on relevant and pressing issues in government."

What Do You Need to Know? voxgov allows users to analyze material generated by government reports on any topic, and to visualize the information using timelines, graphs, and word clouds.

- All of the data updates every 15 to 30 minutes.
- There is live trending of the most active issues in the past 24 hours.
- Measurement of tone of social commentary.
- Everything in the system can be shared legally because it is all public domain.

Key Functions:

Monitor

- All branches of government
- 9,000+ Sources
- ~20k News Docs Daily
- Updated 24×7
- 50+ Document Types

Analyze

Extensive use of data tagging and patented filtering technologies provides unique views and insights including analysis trends over time.

- Data Visualizations
- 52 Timeline Graphs
- Multi-year Comparisons
- Extensive Document Tagging

Track

Keep up to date with custom-built tools that enable easy sharing of valuable information across teams and third parties.

- Custom Feeds
- Save Searches
- Receive Alerts
- Compile Folders
- Generate Reports

Trend voxgov highlights significant changes in issue activity levels coming from within the government conversation throughout the day.

- Multi-Point Trending
- 75 Trending Options
- 15 Minute Updates
- Rapid Drill-Down
- Frequency Monitor

Responsiveness to customer needs

Until now, voxgov was primarily marketed to academic libraries. When Dessau asked me to evaluate the product for a law firm environment, I suggested that the alert features needed to be "fine-tuned" in order to appeal to practicing lawyers who bill by the minute. Lawyers don't want to be overwhelmed with results; they want to see the most relevant materials first and they want to understand *why* a document is relevant to their interests. Within a few weeks, Dessau returned and had implemented almost all the new suggested features, including sorting alert results by relevance, highlighting relevant keywords in alerts, and automatically deduping results (now handled by grouping reissued documents under a single heading). Social media results are also now grouped separately from government releases.

Voxgov is clearly a resource addressing the specialized need of lobbying and government affairs professionals. The product also offers unique materials for researchers and lawyers in any regulatory practice as well as a wide variety of litigation needs. Litigators can use government materials to locate experts, government studies and data to support or dispute facts, as well as to pinpoint the timing of government actions. While the standard legal research systems: Lexis, Westlaw, Bloomberg BNA, and Wolters Kluwer offer the traditional primary sources for statutes and regulations such as the U.S. Code, the CFR, the Federal Register, and the Congressional Records and Congressional Reports, none of them have taken on the development of an archive comparable to that amassed by voxgov.

Law 360 Editorial Team Prepares to Report on Trump Administration Legal Industry Impact

JANUARY 25, 2017

LAW360

In several prior posts I have reported on how legal publishers are preparing to cover the legislative and regulatory impact of the Trump Administration. Scott Roberts, VP and General Manager of Law360 Lexis Legal News, provided the following summary highlighting the Trump Administration issues to be featured in upcoming Law360 newsletters:

Law360 Prepares

The impact of a Trump presidency on the legal industry is likely to be significant and immediate. He has been clear about his desire to roll back, and in some cases completely revamp a slew of regulations, which will likely lead to a serious uptick in legal work as companies work to understand the new rules and head towards implementation and compliance.

As for specifics, Law360 will be closely watching these areas for immediate impact:

Supreme Court nomination: The most memorable impact on the legal community of a Trump presidency is expected to be the configuration of the Supreme Court. With at least one guaranteed Supreme Court justice pick and possibly others to follow over the next four (if not eight) years, President Trump could fundamentally alter the makeup of the Court for decades to come. His picks are expected to be conservative and business friendly.

President Trump has indicated that he will announce his SCOTUS pick within a few weeks following inauguration. Law360 will cover his pick from a number of angles, ranging from the nominee's likelihood of confirmation to the new justice's likely impact on the court's ideological makeup.

Repealing & Replacing the Affordable Care Act: President Trump has vowed to completely overhaul Obamacare, if not do away with it completely. Law360 will be covering the actual process of repealing and replacing the bill on Capitol Hill – and perhaps even more interesting for our readers, we'll cover how the attorneys for health insurers, doctors, hospitals, and all the other people and businesses impacted by the legislation are handling the changes and bracing for the aftermath.

Immigration: This is another area that President Trump had signaled to impact from Day 1 and we'll be watching closely to see how this is approached. In particular, it's expected that he will rescind immigration-related executive orders made by former President Obama. The Deferred Action for Childhood Arrivals program – which protects adults who were brought illegally to the U.S. when they were children – is one that President Trump could jettison right off the bat.

International Trade: President Trump pledged to renegotiate or exit a host of trade agreements, perhaps most notably NAFTA, during his campaign. He's also threatened to impose hefty tariffs on companies that move manufacturing jobs overseas.

EPA & Climate Change: It's also expected that President Trump will likely move to defang the EPA and possibly exit or somehow alter the Paris Agreement on climate change. Environmental issues tend to be highly litigious and many anticipate lawsuits to follow if such efforts are pursued.

While almost no area is "off limits" to potential scrutiny by the incoming Trump administration, Law360 expects these key topics to be the first reforms targeted following [last] Friday's transition of power.

Lex Machina Launches New Apps: Instant Insights into Litigation Damages and Parties

JANUARY 26, 2017

Lex Machina™
a LexisNexis® Company

LexMachina is a system exploding with data. But data doesn't equal insights until you combine elements into a query. Data analysis is pretty new to legal research and Lex Machina is on a mission to keep making it easier for lawyers to extract powerful insights with minimum – as in "no" – training. It also enables lawyers to ask completely new questions.

The Lex Machina system includes hundreds of data elements which can be combined in thousands of permutations. Their modules currently cover: Patent, Trademark, Copyright, Antitrust, ITC, and Securities Litigation.

Today Lex Machina is releasing two important new apps: Damages Explorer, and Parties Comparator, which provide instant insights to litigators. Attorneys can use both apps to quickly model different strategic approaches – using information from the Lex Machina database that previously would have taken weeks to compile using a team of researchers.

Damages Explorer delivers the first-of-its-kind ability to expose, compare, and analyze individual damages awarded. The app can analyze damages awarded by judge, court, and type of damages. Sample reports include:

- Attorneys' fees in a specific district
- Infringement damages awarded by a particular judge

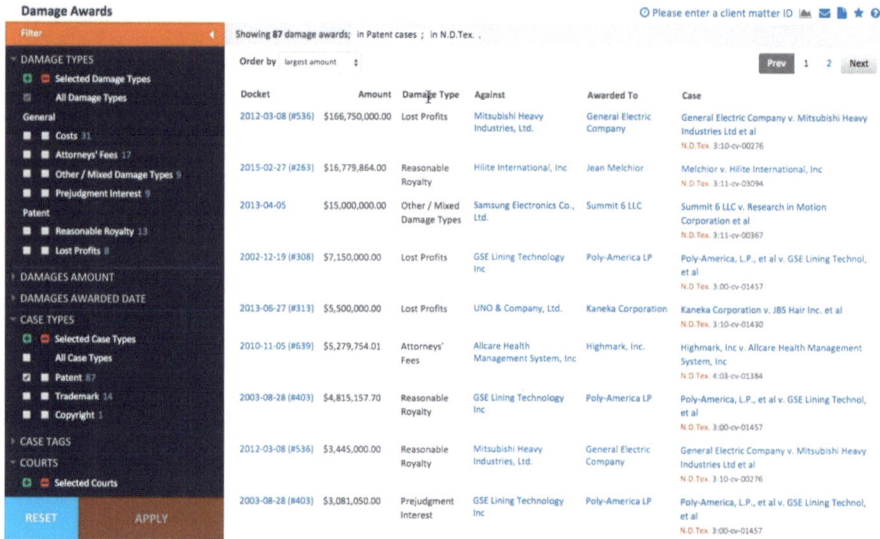

Figure 7: Damages Explorer

According to the press release, Lex Machina has the only complete record of damages awards in patent, copyright, trademark, securities, and antitrust cases since 2009.

Parties Comparator enables lawyers to compare parties across multiple criteria, such as litigation volume, performance, and outcomes. For each party being compared, the application shows damages, remedies, findings won or lost, and case timing milestones.

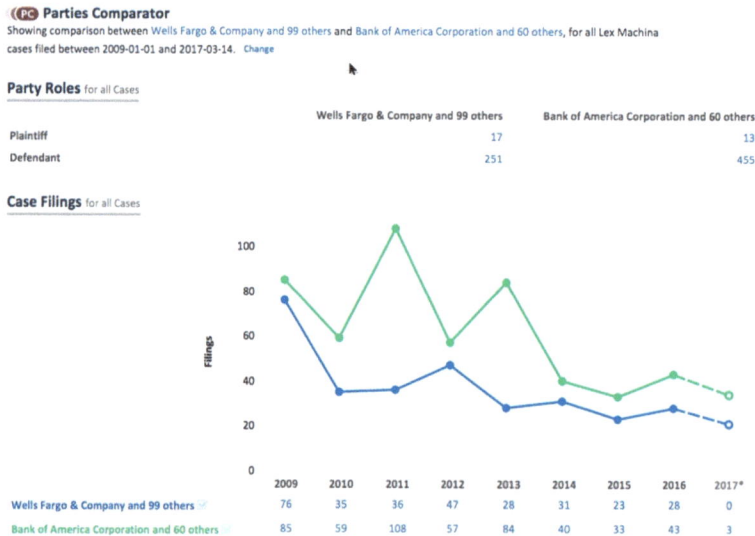

Figure 8: Compare Case Filings by Party

The press release highlights the value of this app as enabling GCs to perform peer benchmarking and for law firms to gain deeper insights into clients and to improve legal strategies.

From the Press Release:

"Today, attorneys need data-driven insights to make sound legal and business decisions. Our new *Damages Explorer* and *Parties Comparator* deliver unprecedented information within seconds instead of days or weeks," said Josh Becker, Lex Machina's CEO. "Being able to easily explore the damages awarded in similar cases, enables attorneys to gauge whether to pursue or settle a case before setting foot in a courtroom. Similarly, the ability to analyze how opposing parties or similar companies have fared in court can give attorneys valuable strategic insights, instant decisioning capabilities, and a distinct competitive advantage."

The Lex Machina Suite of Apps. Lex Machina's previously released *Legal Analytics Apps* (Early Case Assessor, Motion Kickstarter, and Patent Portfolio Evaluator) and *Comparator Apps* (Courts and Judges Comparator and Law Firms Comparator).

MLex: Monitoring Regulatory Convergence and Litigation Risk

FEBRUARY 14, 2017

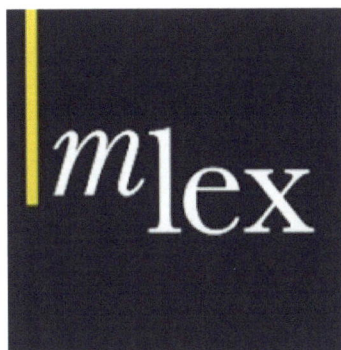

In July 2015 LexisNexis acquired MLex, a newsletter service specializing in international legal analysis of regulatory risk. In recent years MLex has cracked the U.S. market as a "must read" for antitrust lawyers. MLex editors employ an investigative approach combined with in-depth forensic examination of issues by reporters, lawyers, and industry experts located in 15 bureaus around the world. In the last eight months they have launched two new products emerging from vortexes of regulatory uncertainty: Brexit, and the election of Donald Trump. These two newsletters will be examined in Part Two of this post.

The market for specialty news

I recently interviewed MLex founder and CEO, Robert McLeod. MLex has ridden a wave of demand for deep specialized news. McLeod discussed MLex's rise in the context of recent dislocations in the news industry. The Pew Center has documented the decline of the traditional newspapers here: http://assets.pewresearch.org/wp-content/uploads/sites/13/2016/06/30143308/state-of-the-news-media-report-2016-final.pdf.

McLeod witnessed the transformation from inside the traditional news industry where he has deep roots as a professional journalist. He started as a writer with Bloomberg in 1993 when Bloomberg had only 17 reporters in Europe. McLeod focused on antitrust and merger control in Paris, covered energy and investment banking in London, and was promoted to bureau chief in Belgium. McLeod traces his idea for MLex back to 2004. As Internet browsers began eroding the market share of traditional newspapers, the owners of news outlets responded by cutting their most highly compensated reporters – the ones who covered the most complex regulatory and business issues. Newspapers began seeking business and regulatory content from news agencies like Bloomberg and Reuters. There was one catch. Newspaper editors wanted "copy" but they wanted "watered down" versions for general news readers. McLeod recognized that there was still a market for very sophisticated business coverage or as he likes to say, "smart copy."

Since broadband has leveled the playing field. Startups like MLex had a unique opportunity to compete with big news organizations. McLeod left Bloomberg in 2005 to launch MLex.

MLex – "11 Years to Overnight Success"

McLeod filed his first MLex article on July 7, 2005. He recalls celebrating when the first reader clicked on the story. He watched the traffic grow steadily. He found four U.S. law firms who agreed to subscribe for the first year. MLex was not an easy sell. Forty-five firms said they were not interested... they already had a source for all the antitrust news they needed. McLeod was confident, however, he could deliver a product that provided deeper analysis and more compelling content than his competitors.

Over the past decade MLex has branched out to cover financial services, anti-bribery, compliance, data privacy, globalization, and convergence of regulatory risk. McLeod offered an outline which highlights the acceleration of global regulation.

- It took 120 years for antitrust regulation to spread around the world from the U.S.
- It took 40 years for anti-bribery regulation to spread around the world from the U.S.
- It took only 12 years for data privacy and security regulation to go global.

McLeod expects the next big regulatory issue to go global in less than 10 years. All of these regulations expose companies to serious risks, running the gamut from huge fines to jail time for executives. Many of the regulatory regimes are converging and companies which are exposed on one issue may risk exposure on others. This convergence will increase the risk of litigation. According to McLeod, "Companies which operate within multiple jurisdictions will have to update their compliance materials every three months. The job of the global GC is to keep the CEO out of prison."

Today MLex has 85 reporters in 15 bureaus located in key political and financial centers around the globe including Washington, D.C., New York, Sao Paulo, Beijing, Jakarta, and Geneva. Subscribers represent more than 800 law firms and corporations around the globe.

New Issues in the Pipeline

McLeod anticipates that tax and intellectual property will be next areas to experience a surge in global regulation. McLeod also sees opportunity arising from being part of LexisNexis. LexisNexis has a deeper bench of technologists and programmers who can help them add enhancements to the product. McLeod would like to see new visualization features such as regulatory "heatmaps." They plan to offer lawyers the ability to develop custom newsletters on discrete issues that will automatically update. One use case would be shareable pages on specific issues related to a deal.

While library budgets remain tight, specialty news sources for practice groups remain one of the few areas where spending is increasing. Specialty news addresses every lawyer's need to feel smarter than the client, while also responding to every GC's demand that outside counsel follow the business issues facing their industry. Specialty newsletters like MLex are positioned in a market sweet spot where they can simultaneously reduce information anxiety and enhance opportunity.

Up Next: Part Two– MLex Tackles Brexit and The Trump White House

Politics Aside: MLex Offers Straight News Coverage of Brexit and Trump's White House

FEBRUARY 15, 2017

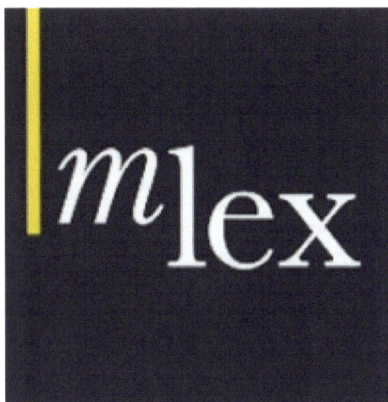

In the past year MLex has launched two "hot topic" newsletters: Brexit Market Insight, and White House Watch, which are positioned at the vortex of regulatory uncertainty and designed to help lawyers and corporate leaders mitigate regulatory risk. I interviewed MLex's founder and CEO Robert McLeod and reported on the evolution of the MLex service and its unique approach covering the global landscape of regulatory risk in an earlier post.

The U.K.'s referendum to exit the European Union and the election of Donald Trump were both surprising outcomes that have roiled the normally somnolent world of regulatory reporting.

Brexit Market Insight

Four months before the majority of British voters approved a referendum to exit the E.U., Robert McLeod began planning a newsletter devoted to "Brexit" – shorthand for British Exit. In a recent interview McLeod recalled that on February 22, 2016, the *Sunday Telegraph* reported that Boris Johnson, the former Mayor of London, journalist, and provocateur had announced his support for Brexit. For the first time McLeod considered the possibility that the Brexit referendum could succeed. McLeod telephoned his co-Founder and Managing

Editor, Duncan Lumsden, to begin discussing the launch of a new product focused on the ramifications of Britain's possible departure from the European Union. The Brexit referendum would be just the first step in a long and uncertain process extending over several years. The U.K. will have to formally invoke "Article 50 of the Lisbon Treaty" which would give Britain and the E.U. two years to agree to the terms of the split. Company executives are facing a prolonged period of uncertainty.

McLeod recognized that business executives and lawyers would be desperate for insights and guidance on a host of issues: What would Brexit mean for their customers, suppliers, competitors, and for individual companies as they plan for the new regulatory environment? They began recruiting writers with special expertise in identifying the regulatory implications of Brexit for their bureaus in London, Paris, Berlin, and Brussels. On June 23, 2016, Britons voted in favor of leaving the E.U. The Brexit product which launched in mid-2016 is updated three or four times per day. The digital newsletter has been profiling the key Brexit players. McLeod recognized that business leaders need to understand who will be influencing and negotiating the new regulatory framework. What are their political beliefs? What are their economic beliefs? Where did they go to school? What speeches have they given? What positions have they taken? According to McLeod there are 900 separate regulations that could possibly be renegotiated... everything from fisheries to footwear could be impacted. To date, *Brexit Market Insights* has been the fastest growing publication in the MLex portfolio.

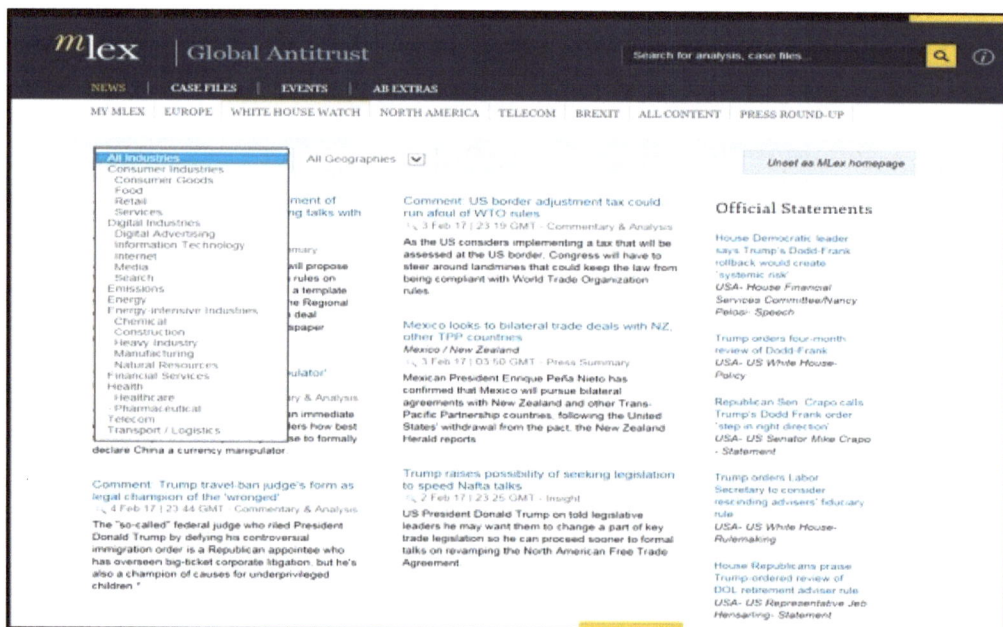

White House Watch Free Until May

The day after Donald Trump won the U.S. presidency, McLeod began pulling resources from around MLex to help him launch a news service to cover the regulatory upheaval promised during Trump's campaign. McLeod is still recruiting journalists with specialized White House experience. Following the Brexit formula, they plan to focus on regulatory issues of interest to corporate leaders, including trade, tax, labor, environment, and energy. McLeod observed that President Trump has up-ended the traditional role of lobbyists and industry associations by engaging directly with company CEOs. MLex editors plans to profile all political appointees in order to better anticipate their regulatory agenda. They had already created profiles of judges on Trump's Supreme Court nominee list.

White House News Without the Politics

McLeod hopes to offer pure legal analysis without a political point of view. If he can pull that off… he will deserve a Pulitzer Prize… and perhaps a new category of Prize!

MLex has eyes and ears around the globe – with news bureaus in 20 major cities. *The White House Watch* will continue to respond to global interest in following the regulatory and legislative impact of the Trump administration. McLeod personally reads coverage of the Trump administration in five major international newspapers and recognized that it is a challenge to sort out the truth. He believes MLex could lead the market in offering White House news, unblemished by hyperbole and partisan rhetoric.

The White House Watch will be free until May. The newsletter can be filtered by regulatory issue to easily locate topics of interest. Lawyers can feel free to distribute stories to their clients.

Thomson Reuters Relaunches Online Treatises: New Formats, Context, and Functionality in Secondary Sources

FEBRUARY 28, 2017

Today Thomson Reuters is announcing the release of re-designed Westlaw Secondary Sources experience. The marketing materials promise that researchers will "start stronger and finish faster." Secondary source content includes more than 4,000 treatises, encyclopedias, and serials, including titles such as the iconic Wright and Miller on *Federal Practice and Procedure, Corpus Juris Secundum, American Jurisprudence 2d,* state practice guides including Rutter, and even *Black's Law Dictionary.*

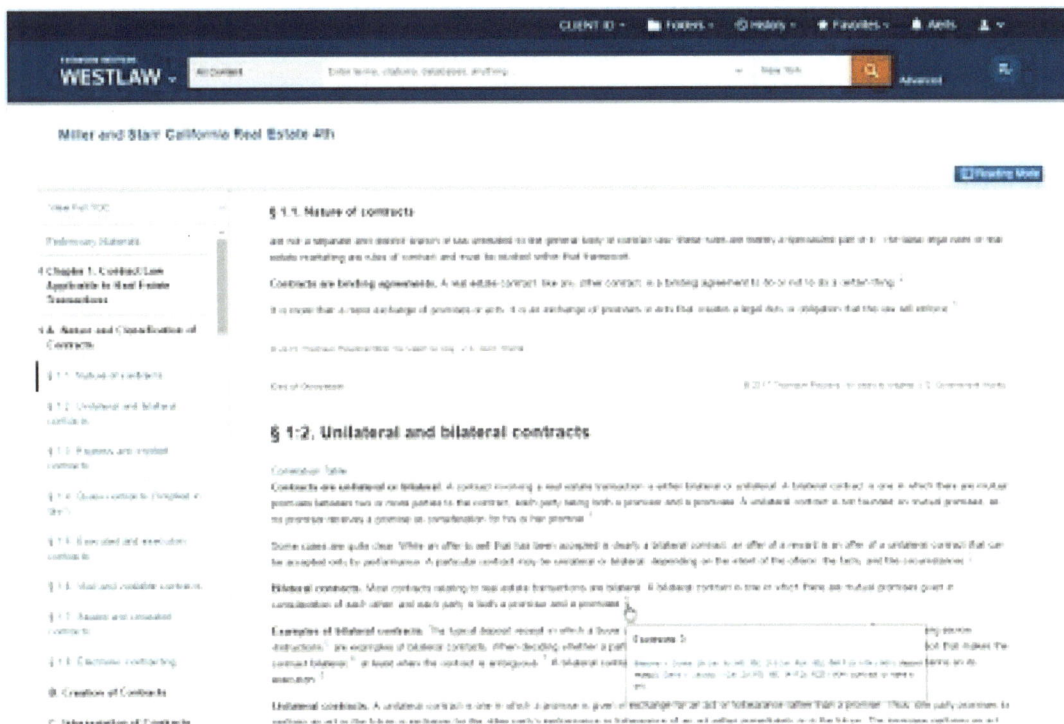

Figure 9: Treatises offer interactive Table of Contents

This is not a new product. It is an upgrade that all Westlaw subscribers will experience when they select secondary sources in Westlaw. This new display format will also appear for users who access treatises using CUIs "custom user interfaces."

When I first became a reference librarian, I experienced the West treatises in the "bad old days" before case law was fully digitized. I noted with frustration that the indices to West treatises were hierarchical – meaning you could not search directly for the word "rescission," you had to know that it was a type of contract remedy – and you would leaf through the index hoping to stumble across the right subcategory. In other words, you had to already know about the subject in order to learn more about it.

The digitization of treatises has enhanced keyword access while reducing precision. The enhancements offered by the new secondary source filters and navigation tools improve focus and precision of results. As many law firm partners, professors, and law librarians worry that young lawyers are unfamiliar with the major treatises in each legal subject area, the enhancements of Westlaw secondary sources should drive up associates' exposure to and use of major treatises. Every legal publisher including Thomson Reuters is focused on enhancements which support the client demand for lawyer efficiency – getting lawyers to the best insights and relevant content in the fewest clicks!

Megan Riley, a product developer at Thomson Reuters, provided an advance demo for me. According to their press release, secondary sources are the second most heavily used content type on Westlaw, following case law. Riley highlighted the fact that the new enhancements will free researchers from the constrictions of a linear research path. The goal is to enable users to more quickly identify, filter, and interact with relevant resources. The impact is that the experience of searching across the entire repository of secondary sources and the search and navigation within individual resources is dramatically improved.

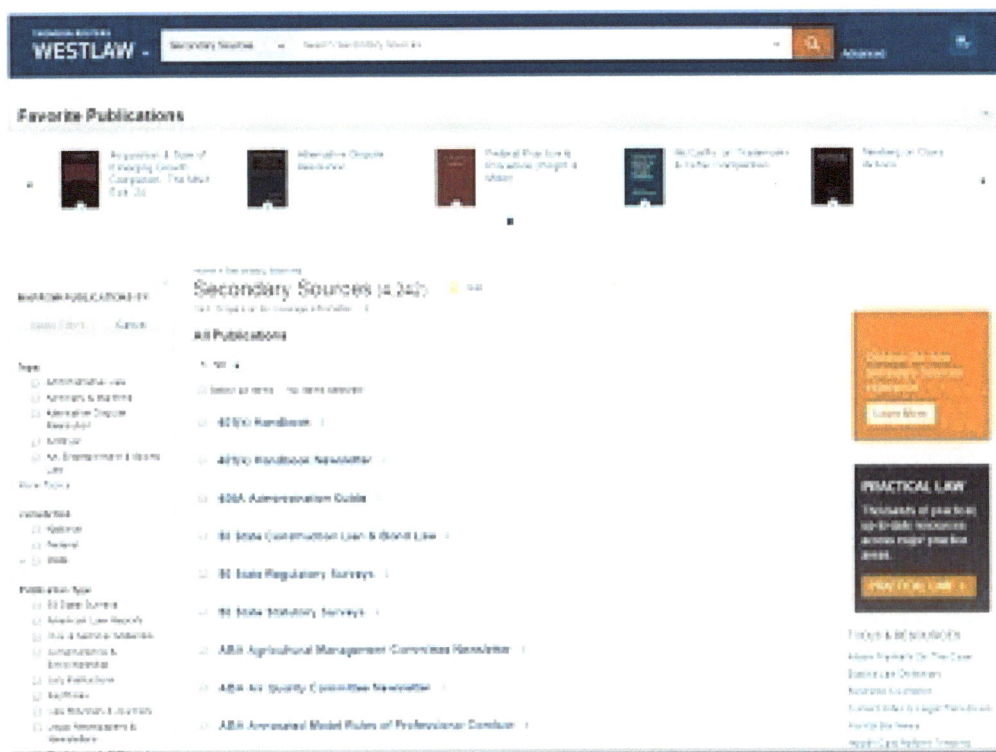

Figure 10: Favorite Publications Display

New features include:

- Streamlined navigation, browsing with enhanced access to contextual materials.
- Cleaner, more intuitive look and feel.
- Search across all secondary sources with filters which can be combined to enhance precision, such as targeting California resources addressing zoning laws.
- "Reading mode" enables researchers to scroll through multiple documents in a single display. This mode is for reading only – printing is not supported in this mode.
- Scope screens provide a quick overview of key relevant factors regarding content and updating and include links to related sources.
- Search results display related documents as additional options for a researcher to explore.
- A research trail persists across the top of the page.
- Favorite publications can be selected and displayed in a bookshelf like format at the top of the screen displaying familiar "book cover" icons.

- Rutter publications will include pinpoint linking to enable navigation directly to a referenced citation rather than current process of scrolling.

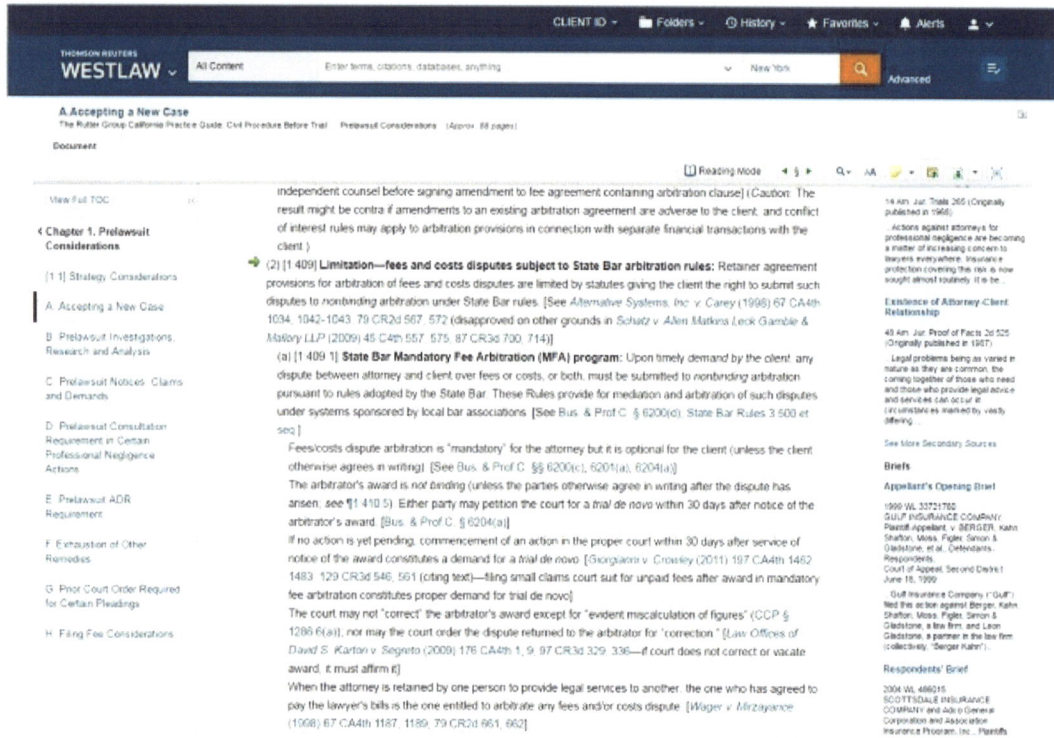

Figure 11: Rutter Materials offer Pinpoint Linking

The U.S. secondary source redesign is the first of a global redesign plan. Redesigns of WestlawUK and WestlawNext Canada secondary sources will follow. I queried whether this enhancement to secondary sources within Westlaw signaled a change in their eBook strategy. I was told it did not – they remain committed to their Proview eBook platform.

A Few Humble Suggestions:

The new tables of contents feature are a big improvement, but I have a few suggestions:

- Add an "expand all" feature rather than having to expand topic by topic.
- Add an "updated as of" notation adjacent to titles when searching for a source – this will enable a searcher to quickly determine the most current resource, bypassing the need to check individual scope notes after selecting a publication.

- Since users remain concerned about client charges, I think it would be a good idea to have a single print charge for viewing any document in a chapter rather than triggering a series of charges from reviewing different parts of a chapter.

LexisNexis Sued by Law Firm Alleging Breach of Contract, Deceptive Practices for Selling Codes with Omissions and Errors

MARCH 1, 2017

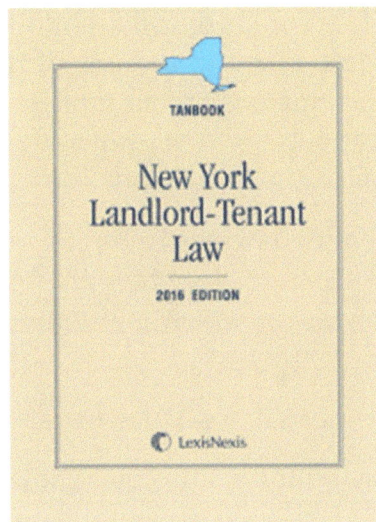

Today the Courthouse News Service reported that the law firm Himmelstein McConnell, Gribben Donahue and Joseph LLP filed a class action lawsuit against Matthew Bender & Company, a Member of LexisNexis Group, Inc., in a New York State Supreme Court on February 23rd (http://www.courthousenews.com/ class-calls-lexisnexis-publication-totally-useless/).

The complaint alleges that the annual publication, the New York Landlord Tenant Law book, includes 37 textual omissions and 18 inaccuracies. According to the complaint, the publication also known as the "Tanbook" is sold as a "compilation of all the laws and regulations governing landlord tenant matters in New York, providing the text of state statutes and regulations and local laws," and contains serious errors and omissions which render it "of no value to the attorneys, laypeople or judges who use it." The omissions as identified in the complaint appear to be very significant – entire paragraphs of text on issues such as rent control are missing from the "Tanbook."

The class action represents everyone who has purchased a "Tanbook" in the past six years and accuses Matthew Bender of breach of contract, unjust enrichment, and engaging in deceptive business practices, and seeks refunds, compensatory damages, and an injunction to prevent Matthew Bender from engaging in future deceptive business practices.

The "Tanbook" which costs between $100-120 per volume, is part of a suite of annual desk books also known as color books used by lawyers in New York State.

I am personally on a quest to reduce purchases of desk books as much as possible. The cost of annual disposable volumes of code mounts up in a large firm. A firm with hundreds of lawyers could spend hundreds of thousands of dollars. Most firms end up purchasing the same content in multiple formats: online, eBooks, hardback print statutory compilations, and annual desk books. Paperback codes are at the bottom of the publication "food chain."

I am a big advocate for migrating lawyers to digital versions of codes which are inherently more current and accurate since they are updated throughout the year rather than fixed in a print version which is often out of date on the day it is shipped out to purchasers.

Are There Errors in Other Lexis Publications?

The big question is... are these editorial problems contained to this one particular publication or does it signal a larger systemic issue impacting other books in the series or other Lexis publications?

Even more concerning is the prospect that the same errors might reside in their online services. One would expect publishers to maximize editorial efficiency by maintaining a "master" version of each statute in digital format which is updated as laws and regulations change and which can be repurposed in other hardbound, paperback, and eBook versions of each code.

The risks to lawyers in relying on a statute which is missing code sections cannot be overstated.

Lexis is Not the First and Won't be the Last to Discover Errors in Publications

However, LexisNexis executives need to reach out to their subscribers and provide assurances that they are engaged in a thorough investigation of the extent of the problem and address how and when they will correct the errors. Last year Thomson Reuters disclosed that they had discovered "non material" case law errors in hundreds of cases. They controlled the "bad news" by issuing a press release and posting updates on their website about how they were identifying and correcting the errors. I urge LexisNexis executives to take a similar open approach with their customers in order to provide both the assurances and actions to address editorial problems identified in their digital and print publications.

LexisNexis Responds to My Post About the "Tanbook" Errors Litigation

MARCH 6, 2017

I received an official response from Ashley Jefferson, Senior Communication Specialist at LexisNexis, regarding my recent post regarding the lawsuit filed against LexisNexis claiming that the statutory compilation of Landlord Tenant laws known as the "Tanbook" contains material errors and omissions.

Here is the official statement:

> We understand your concern about the legal publications you use.
>
> While LexisNexis does not comment on pending litigation, we can tell you that the subject of this litigation (a Matthew Bender publication known as the "Tanbook") has no connection with or effect on the online legal research solutions available from LexisNexis, including Lexis Advance.
>
> LexisNexis is committed to delivering high-quality products and services. To that end, we apply multiple-step editorial processes across our full portfolio, always striving to deliver to customers the quality legal content they rely on to be successful.

Rumor of the Day: Is Ravel Law Being Bought by LexisNexis? Another Acquisition Without Integration?

MARCH 10, 2017

LexisNexis has been on an extraordinary spree – buying up companies that are almost always the brainchild of a former lawyer and always the product of entrepreneurial inspiration and grit. The latest opportunity? Target? Victim? May be Ravel Law... Sources in the legal publishing industry are whispering that LexisNexis is about to acquire Ravel Law. I reached out to Daniel Lewis, CEO of Ravel Law, and he politely responded with a "no comment."

This would signal that LexisNexis is trying to dominate the legal analytics market the way they have grown to dominate the legal news market. Will *Justly* be next?

Lexis Content Acquisition Strategy?

For the past few years LexisNexis has been collecting legal content gems – Law360, Lex Machina, MLex, Knowledge Mosaic. Instead of integrating them into the massive LexisNexis organization, each company has remained a stand-alone operation retaining their entrepreneurial culture, their key talent, and their client relationships. The company has stated that core Lexis content is being leveraged to enhance the offering of the smaller companies. This is a reasonable short-term strategy. At some point Lexis should start aligning some of the content synergies to transform the old Lexis workhorse. Are they ready to do that?

The concern I have is that Lexis is collecting without integrating and streamlining. True, they were showing off a limited integration of Lex Machina and Lexis at Legal Tech. This integration allows lawyers to see some analytics with their Lexis search results.

Is the "Tanbook" Litigation a Canary in the Coal Mine? Has Lexis Extended Itself Too Far?

I remember "Total Quality Management" business guru Tom Peters once commenting that companies must have a culture of quality. Coffee stains on the airline food trays suggest there might be something wrong with engine maintenance. Maybe not logical, but the "Tanbook" litigation issue does raise the flag of whether Lexis as a company can maintain the quality across their extended product lines. Most baffling is that Lexis asserted in an email to me that the "color books" are being created outside of Lexis. Think about that – they are not using the massive Lexis data streams which include updates of state statutes and regulations to assure that their annual statutory codes are kept up-do-date. I have visions of people with glue sticks pasting amended regulations over the old ones. Not a 21st-century process. It begs the question "why?"

Why Don't They Integrate and Build the Ultimate "Legal Research Service?"

This is the most baffling issue to me. LexisNexis has terrific assets that if combined could be game changing... I understand wanting to keep the revenue from all of the legacy products, but there is no evidence of an intent to integrate them into a more powerful LexisNexis platform.

Augmented Intelligence as a Reference Librarian? Twice as Fast, Half as Good... For Now...

MARCH 30, 2017

Last night I delivered the Gillard Lecture at the St. John's University Graduate Division of Library and Information Science. My presentation was titled "Has the Librarian-ship Sailed? Redefining the Profession in a Post Google World." I want to thank the program director Professor James Vorbach for the wonderful reception. It was great to see a contingent of my LLAGNY friends who made the trek out to the Queens campus in the driving rain. And then there was the inevitable technology glitch... an encrypted flash drive that would not run part of my presentation.

So Here it Is... The Missing "Wow Moment" of My Presentation

This Ted Institute video of Gil Dario on cognitive computing provides a jaw dropping scenario in which a Watson-enabled computer is responding to the types of complex business research questions which are fairly routine in a "big law" research environment. In this video two business analysts are asking Watson to pinpoint companies matching specific criteria, industry, revenue, size. Watson can automatically populate a table with data after digesting a policy document. But there is one major difference... between Watson and a research specialist. (https://www.youtube.com/watch?v=oheqP8d6vtQ)

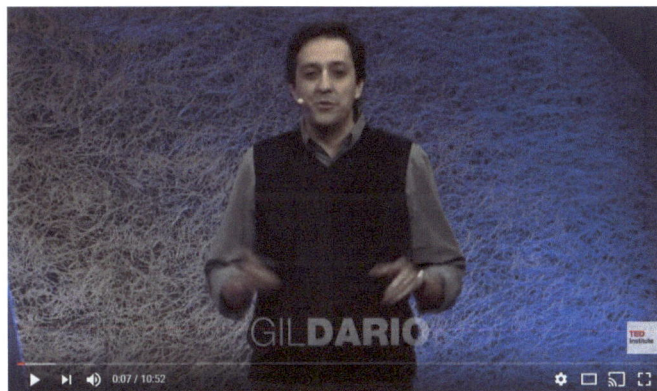

Figure 12: Gil Dario TedTalk

What About the Contextualizing Questions?

I intended to use the video to launch a discussion about how Watson's performance compared to a live researcher. What would the future role be for Watson? A replacement for the research team, or as an adjunct "member" of the team?

Complex research is a dialog. Researchers not only answer questions, they ask them! This "Socratic dialog" helps focus the requester on issues which provide important context for narrowing and focusing the research.

Without Big Data Skillsets, Big Data Could Generate Big Noise

Large data sets will play an increasingly important role in making new strategic insights available to law firms. As illustrated in the video, augmented intelligence will speed the analysis once the data is identified. But someone has to select and vet the data. Information professionals possess the skillset required for making sure that "big data" is also "good data."

Here is a short list of those skills:

- The ability to locate the best and most appropriate data at the lowest cost.
- The ability to assess the quality of external data sources. All information is not of equal quality. The temptation to harvest free open source data could put a firm at risk especially if the data were used in advising clients.
- The ability to assess the provenance of the data. Is the data from a primary source? Or has it been handled and altered? By whom and how?
- Expert knowledge of, or ability to determine the reputation of the data source. Is it known to be a reliable source?
- The ability to interview the requester and help them to define the scope and limits of their need.
- The ability to query the data and uncover patterns which suggest the need to ask more questions or pursue additional lines of inquiry.

Will the Future Give Rise to the Chief Query Officer?

Let's face it...

In a Big Data world, everyone will potentially have access to the same data.

In a Big Data world, advantage will be gained by asking better questions.

In a Big Data world, every firm will be striving to be one question ahead of the competition.

...And it will need to be the right question!

So will this give rise to the Chief Query Officer?

Start/Stop Poll Results: Ravel Law Analytics Voted Best New Product – Lexis Search Term Mapping Best New Feature – ROI Tracking and Research Workflow Tools Emerge as Leading Workflow Enhancement Products

MARCH 31, 2017

In December, I offered readers the opportunity to respond to the 2016 Start/Stop Poll in which they could vote for the best new products and features, and highlight the products they planned to say good-bye to. The results of the process part of the survey are posted here: https://deweybstrategic.lexblogplatform.com/2017/04/the-wisdom-of-colleagues-plea-for-prin.

For the second year in a row Ravel Law Analytics has won the Dewey B Strategic Readers "Start/Stop Poll" for best new product. Lex Machina's New Securities Module placed second. Ravel Law tied for best product in 2015 with Wolters Kluwer's Cheetah search platform.

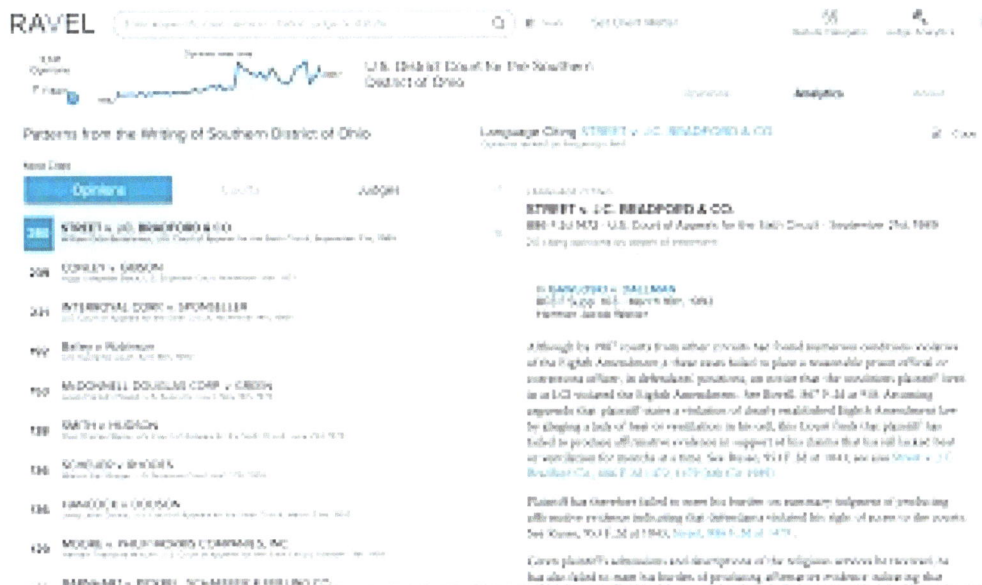

Figure 13: Ravel Law's Court Analytics

Additional products (in alphabetical order) nominated by readers include:

- Audit Analytics
- D&B Onboard
- Docket Navigator which is actually a patent analytics product
- CARA from Casetext which reviews documents for missing precedent
- Cheetah – Wolters Kluwer's new platform replacing IntelliConnect which tied for first place last year
- iPad Pro 9.7/Pencil
- Lex Machina's Securities Module
- LitIQ – linguistic analysis of documents
- Luminance for product review and due diligence
- Newsdesk – the LexisNexis news aggregation and curation platform
- Practice Point

What was the best FEATURE/FUNCTION added to an information resource in 2016?

Lexis Search Term Mapping and navigation bar was voted best new feature added to an existing product.

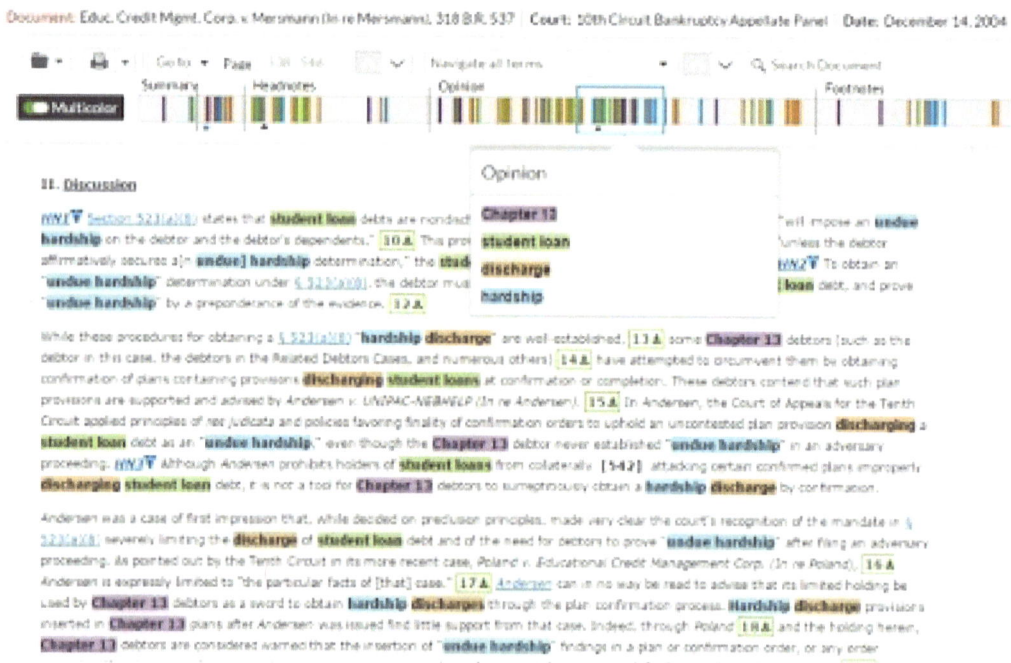

Figure 14: LexisNexis Search Term Mapping

Additional features recommended by readers:

- PDFs of significant complaints included in Court Wire emails for attorney self-service
- "GRAB A" from Bloomberg Professional
- Lex Machina Apps
- Westlaw Answers
- Practice Point
- Bloomberg Law's new business intelligence and analytics platform
- Lexis Predictive Legislation

What PRODUCT did your department/organization STOP using in 2016 or plan to stop in 2017?

The perennial products on the chopping block are print materials as well as the high-ticket Westlaw and Lexis enterprise contracts. As these constructs come up for renewal, law firms grapple with the challenge of cancelling one and relying exclusively on the other vendor. Only one respondent reported taking the sole online provider plunge by cancelling their enterprise Lexis contract in 2016.

Law firm budgets remain flat. The easiest way to bring in a new and innovative product is to cancel an existing subscription. The variety of products listed below suggests to me that resources monitoring platforms have enabled the surgical targeting of under-performing products. Information professionals are taking an active role in the strategic management of digital resources.

- VC Experts
- Hoover's
- RefTraker
- InfoNgen (news aggregation platform)
- West KM
- CCH Cheetah
- Practical Law
- Lexis Publisher (moved to NewsDesk)
- Courthouse News Service Jumbo
- Checkpoint
- ROSS
- Debtwire
- Intelligize
- Capital IQ

What NEW INFORMATION/WORKFLOW PRODUCTS do you expect to be rolled out in your organization in 2017?

Electronic Resource Management products (Research Monitor and Onelog and Research workflow products (Quest and Reftraker) were the two categories of products mentioned most often as 2017 product implementation to improve workflow.

Additional initiatives include:

- We are looking at KM products
- We have purchased a new intranet product and will be rolling it out in 2017
- Enterprise Proview for desk books from Thomson Reuters
- Adding more Law360 modules
- BigSquare
- Single sign-on/SSO/SAML for a variety of our legal research products, to eliminate the need for lawyers to have to enter credentials
- Lex Machina Antitrust Smart Tasks
- Kira
- Research Hub
- Clarion BNA convergence dashboards
- NewsDesk
- I'm working on posting some of my technology sessions online using Panopto's new quizzing feature
- Courtroom Insights
- iManage – Document management system

What product would you most like to see developed in Legal information technology area?

Improved access to litigation analytics from both state and federal courts with enhanced coding to improve strategic insights emerged as the leading product demanded by information professionals.

- Access to all state court documents online, similar to PACER. But better, and preferably free.
- I would love a way to be able to search across all the platforms we subscribe to, but I would even settle for a way to locate specific titles or products via a search. As long as that search doesn't require us to catalog a vendor's entire offerings!

- State court complaints and dockets are coming online too slowly. Disruption would be welcome in this category.
- More transparent search engines.
- We need a better financial system for tracking our expenses that goes deeper than our firm's financial system allows. An invoice often contains many titles, a mix of print and electronic, a mix of book versus subscription, and a mix of individual and department users. We need a system that enables us to track *and report* at the granular level, preferably one that ties to Research Monitor usage and includes contract images, contract terms, licensed user info, and more.
- A litigation landscape tool that would allow you to more easily identify the high value cases (as opposed to the commoditized work) pertaining to a particular company. Lex Machina and Bloomberg are heading in that direction.
- An easy-to-use "know your client" product that can produce reports and be used by "non-researchers."
- Something that searches across all of our online subscriptions.
- A low-cost news aggregator that provides info law schools need (and that we can afford).
- I would like to see companies continue to improve access to dockets that have not been electronically filed and at reasonable cost.
- Easier classification of emails into the document management system.
- A biometric device that will eliminate passwords.
- Analytics.

What is your favorite app for personal use? (What do you use it for if it has multiple functions?)

- Shazam
- PocketCasts. I can organize podcasts by category (fun and work-related), sort and play podcasts set at specific speeds
- Words with Friends
- MTA bus time
- Waze
- Every Dollar
- Google maps
- Kindle app
- Selfie Editor
- Tile app
- Asana – online team and task management

- Pinterest
- Pokemon Go
- Find iPhone
- Gas Buddy locates gas stations and prices on a map

Thanks to everyone who took the time to share their wisdom and insights with their colleagues.

The Wisdom of Colleagues: A Plea for Print – KM, Curation, Outreach, and ROI Top Process Initiatives in Start/Stop Process Survey

APRIL 3, 2017

Today I am summarizing the process initiatives submitted by readers responding to the Start/Stop Poll.

The 2016-17 initiatives focus on: visibility outreach, targeted marketing, lawyer training, and collecting attorney feedback and measuring value and satisfaction with resources and services. The most surprising response was a plea for the retention of print resources.

Could we have reached the end of "the end of print?"

I have been reading a book called *The Revenge of Analog* (David Sax, Public Affairs: 2016) which offers a fascinating catalog of "dead" analog formats which are being revived and re-positioned in new higher end niche markets: phonographic records, 35-millimeter film, and yes... print magazines and books. Today my Sunday *Washington Post* – yes, I read a paper newspaper – included a new "Weekly TV Guide." I thought they eliminated the TV Guide over 10 years ago.

And then... I discovered in this year's survey responses a plea to slow the relentless elimination of print. "Stop eliminating print treatises that lawyers want to read the old-fashioned way. Enough of the architects and finance people driving this. Our associates want print copies of the best books, and research shows that full absorption of knowledge is best achieved when reading print media."

While every firm is at a different stage of migration from print to digital, some firms may have reached the bone – there is no more to cut. Other firms will continue to eliminate print – but perhaps print will stabilize. There will be a core set of resources that will be deemed by firms and practices as necessary and worth the cost and the overhead.

Describe any ORGANIZATIONAL (task/process/initiative) that you STOPPED in 2016 or plan to STOP in 2017?

- We stopped buying about 50% more of our print collection.
- We stopped using RefTracker as we found it no longer worked for us and are looking at other ways to track reference requests.
- KF call numbers.
- Posting upcoming training sessions on our SharePoint page (No one ever read them.)
- We stopped creating a separate "classes with online materials" page on the law school website.
- Since we have reduced our collection, we no longer have a need to outsource our filing.
- No longer keeping any ABA periodicals in print.
- Retired our legacy news delivery home-grown service.
- Research team to focus on complex research. All document retrieval to be handled by paraprofessional team.
- Stopped daily review of new cases files.
- Stopped doing new client intake research for new business department.

Describe any ORGANIZATIONAL (task/process/initiative) that you STARTED in 2016.

- We began analyzing usage of Courthouse News and its effectiveness in acquiring new business.
- Improved data tracking of invoices to better see practice group allocation of resources.

- Started tracking filing time/budget by title to target high maintenance print resources.
- Started to revamp desk book distribution methods in effort to turn some titles digital.
- Expanded the content and number of Lexis Advance Resource Centers (eLibraries).
- More streamlined accounting.
- We added several more custom curated newsletters for practice groups.
- Switched news aggregation platform.
- Systematic procedures to "market" the library's services using "triggers" such as a new client, lawyer promotion.
- We started getting in front of attorneys more. Our plan is to do a ton of travel in 2017.
- Replacing Manzama with EOS.
- We've started including the clinic in our technology lectures.
- Enhanced data collection.
- Supporting legal project manager.
- Competitive Intelligence team moved from Marketing to Research and Knowledge team.
- Litigation History Checklist Legal Research Competencies Self-Assessment Tool (based on AALL competencies).

Describe any ORGANIZATIONAL (task/process/initiative) you plan to START in 2017.

- Legal Research Platform RFP eLearning Modules.
- Adding a 4-question survey to responses to requests, encouraging customers to comment on our service.
- We are looking into KM and also how to possibly apply AI to our practices.
- Re-vamp the intranet and increase the library's offerings of practice-group specific resource links and suggested research starting points.
- Creating an internal knowledge repository for the library.
- Writing procedure and policy manuals and cross training staff.
- We are starting to drive use to specific online resources over print on a practice group basis.
- Improve real-time client pages using Thomson Reuters Intelligence Center.
- Knowledge platform revamp.
- Focus will be on a number of knowledge management tools that bring efficiency to the practice.

- Launch a new firm Intranet.
- Launch SmartTasks.
- Launch LexisNewDesk and BNA Convergence dashboards.
- Relaunch a newly envisioned Knowledge services bulletin.
- Move off CNS dockets to Bloomberg Enterprise dockets/Westlaw Dockets.
- Install Research Hub.
- We plan to start including the incubatees in our technology lectures.
- Redesign our library's Intranet page.
- Space planning.
- Reboot KM.
- Migrate from RefTracker to Quest.
- Making more presentations to practice groups and surveying the attorneys to find out what they use the most and what they would like to learn.
- GeniePlus [Lucidea product] library management system. Upgrading from Inmagic DBTextWorks.
- All document retrieval shifted away from research specialists and sent to document retrieval team in low cost center.

Bloomberg Law Releases Data Compliance Risk Benchmark Tool and Report Identifying High Risk Countries

APRIL 20, 2017

Yesterday Bloomberg Law released an important new feature in the Bloomberg Law: Privacy & Data Security product called the Compliance Risk Benchmarks tool. The tool ranks the "burden" and compliance risks in 47 countries. South Korea tops the list of data breach notification compliance risk earning a score of 87 out of 100.

Bloomberg Law also released a related report, "Anticipating the Burden of Risk," which provides an overview of the international regulatory environment and the risk landscape surrounding breach notification compliance. The report features an analysis of the countries with the highest compliance risk for breach notification, with write-ups on the top five countries, which include South Korea, Colombia, Mexico, France, and Japan. (http://images.about.bna.com/Web/ BloombergBNA/%7B478c7f24-f919-49b5-9def-c2d72e4a7626%7D_LEGAL_ WP_Compliance_Risk_Benchmarks_BRAVO.pdf)

What is the Compliance Risk Benchmark?

The tool is designed to assist outside and inside counsel, and compliance professionals in assessing data compliance risk around the world. To accomplish this they have created a risk score based on eight risk factors analyzed using a proprietary algorithm. *Compliance Risk Benchmarks* compares the burdens and risks related to ten topics impacting global businesses including data security, data transfer, online privacy, and employee monitoring and surveillance.

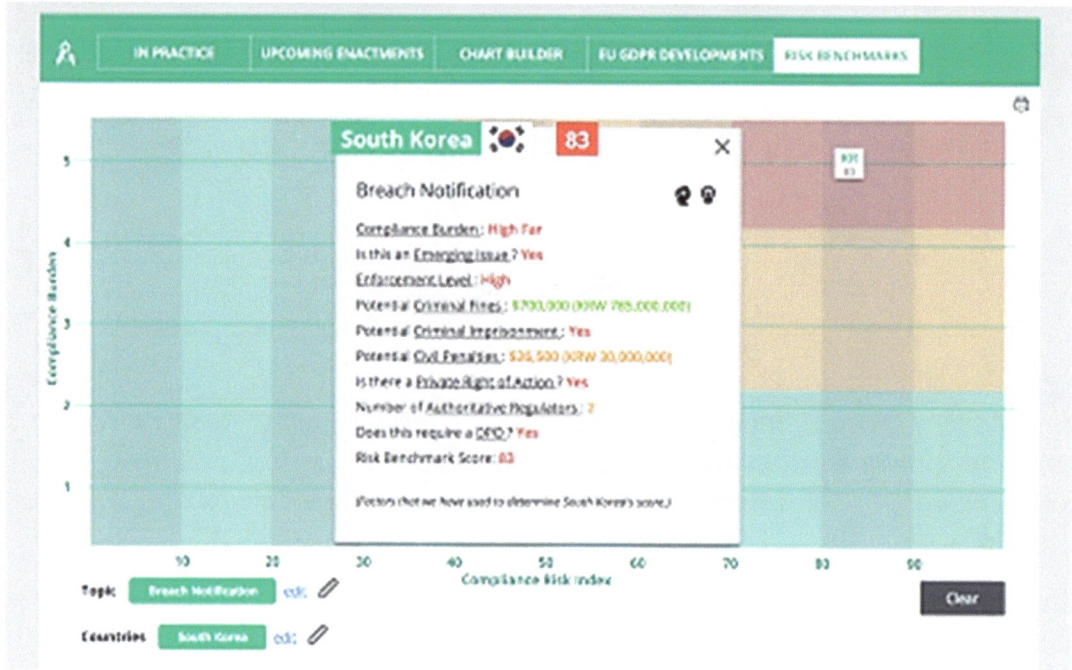

Figure 15: Bloomberg Law's Risk Benchmark

The new tool and data provide a relative risk score for each country based on measures including:

- Enforcement level
- Potential monetary penalties
- Imprisonment
- Litigation exposure

The Compliance Risk

Compliance Risk Benchmarks incorporates expert analysis from data protection professionals in each country as well as news and relevant laws and regulations from 55 countries with its robust data visualization feature. Users can also go from viewing multiple countries to a snapshot of each country's risk factors. Comparative charts can be generated to show legal requirements for key issues such as: employee health information, online privacy, personnel records, electronic marketing, data transfer, employee background checks, employee monitoring and surveillance, data security, data collection, and processing.

Algorithms and Visualization

The score is generated by a proprietary Bloomberg BNA algorithm and offers subscribers a wide range of interactive comparative charts. Upcoming legislation charts displays the status of proposed legislation and regulation across jurisdictions.

E.U. Compliance

Additional features in the platform include the E.U. GDPR development timeline which provides access to legislative history, analysis and guidance on the complex E.U. data privacy laws and regulations.

Access

All Bloomberg Law subscribers now have full access to the benchmarking tool. Bloomberg Law: Privacy & Data Security is also available as a stand-alone product. Additional information regarding the product and contact information is available in the press release at:

https://www.multivu.com/players/English/8062531-bloomberg-law/?c=y

Casetext's CARA Launches New "Brief Finder" Feature

MAY 17, 2017

Only weeks after receiving the prestigious 2017 New Product Award from the American Association of Law Libraries, CARA is announcing today the release of a new "Brief Finder" feature.

Casetext's CARA (Case Analysis Research Assistant) launched with the promise of helping lawyers find the most relevant case law. Last August I reviewed CARA in a post: Citation Fingerprint, Celestial Footnotes and Opinion Sourcing: Casetext Launches CARA (http://deweybstrategic.blogspot.com/2016/08/cara.html).

According to its press release, Brief Finder promises to surface the most relevant legal briefs filed in federal courts "by the county's best law firms... With no extra work, litigators gain unprecedented visibility into how world-class attorneys have argued the same issues they are working on, giving CARA users an extraordinary competitive edge."

Jake Heller, founder and CEO of Casetext, notes that "Every lawyer knows that the best way to find good arguments is to look to your peers – other great attorneys who have taken on the same issues and researched them thoroughly. But finding the right brief is hard and expensive. CARA Brief Finder makes finding these invaluable resources effortless. The Casetext VP of Legal Research, Pablo Arredondo underscores the editorial effort they put in to selecting briefs from only the largest firms, specialty boutiques, and government agencies. "We started with hundreds of thousands of briefs and culled this down to tens of thousands of briefs from highly reputable sources."

Use Cases. The press release highlights the following use cases:

- Predicting opposing counsel's arguments based on what similarly situated litigants have argued. By running drafts through CARA, CARA Brief Finder will surface previously filed briefs that both oppose and support a litigator's arguments. See how other leading attorneys have approached the same issue you're tackling right now – within seconds.
- Making sure litigators don't leave out any arguments. Review briefs filed by peers in the legal community to ensure you are not missing a key argument and that you've articulated those arguments as effectively as possible.
- Helping litigators draft the most compelling briefs efficiently. Quickly and efficiently assemble the information litigators need to provide best-in-class service to clients.

First Low-Cost Provider to Offer Briefs. Although premium services Westlaw, Lexis, and Bloomberg Law have offered a Briefs database for years, Casetext maybe the first low-cost provider to offer searchable access to briefs, and they are certainly the first to offer access using an advanced algorithm to determine relevance.

Access. Existing CARA subscribers will have access to "Brief Finder" for the duration of their subscription term at no additional charge. The CARA Brief Finder will be a separate module which can be added for an additional charge.

I recently had the opportunity to ask Arredondo a few questions about how CARA has evolved over the past year:

How many firms are on board?

We currently have deals with ten large law firms and dozens of smaller firms, in addition to hundreds of solo practitioners. Casetext attracts over 1 million unique users to our site on a monthly basis.

What has your growth been like?

Casetext has grown substantially over the last several months in three key ways: (1) we are growing our team, from engineers and data scientists, to account managers, (2) we raised a $12M Series B round of venture funding (the largest round ever by a legal research company) and we are actively deploying those resources to continue to create innovative, effective products that attorneys can immediately start using in practice, and (3) in a short period of time we have sold subscriptions of our flagship product offering, CARA, to key firms across the country while expanding our presence to 75 law schools across the country.

We decided early on to make CARA freely available to the courts. Judges and clerks all over the country, both federal and state, appellate and trial, have started using CARA and we have been very encouraged by the early response. At a training at one circuit court, the clerks were emphatic that litigants almost invariably overlook relevant case law.

How has the product evolved?

The early and enthusiastic adoption of CARA by courts and law firms has given us great user feedback, which has guided the evolution of the product. One of the most critical improvements has been combining the power of CARA with keyword queries. Currently CARA defaults to showing the top fifteen recommendations for the brief as a whole. Attorneys interested in just one specific issue can easily enhance the search with a keyword query without losing all of the context-specific analysis that CARA provides.

The other major improvement in the platform is that CARA now returns briefs as well as case law. Our users are very excited about this and so are we. Briefs can be one of the most expensive databases to access on traditional platforms. We get these briefs from PACER; it is important to understand that we never store, much less use, the briefs that attorneys upload for research. In order to ensure quality, we have culled our brief database (which updates regularly) down to briefs filed by leading law firms, boutiques, non-profits, and government agencies. You can filter the briefs by jurisdiction or use narrow-by-keyword.

Last year, I met Arredondo when he approached me in a meeting room at the AALL Conference in Chicago and asked me to see a brief demo of CARA. This year Arredondo reports that Casetext will have a booth in the Exhibit Hall at the AALL conference in Austin this July. Congratulations to Heller and Arredondo and all the folks at Casetext on the AALL award and the Brief Finder launch. I am reminded of an advertising slogan from the 70s: "You've come a long way, baby."

View the CARA Brief Finder Press Release at:

https://www.businesswire.com/news/home/20170517005306/en/casetext-Unveils-CARA-Finder

Wolters Kluwer On a Roll: New Cybersecurity Product, Enhanced Arbitration Platform and ktMINE IP Alliance

MAY 19, 2017

The Wolters Kluwer product development teams have been busy. In recent months they have announced a reboot of their International Arbitration product, launched a Cybersecurity product and entered into an alliance enabling them to offer ktMINE IP analytics through the Cheetah platform.

Cyber security

Wolters Kluwer has taken on one of the hottest topics in law and policy with the launch of a new Cybersecurity and Privacy Law Suite. The product tracks regulatory developments and provides a comprehensive overview of the global regulatory landscape.

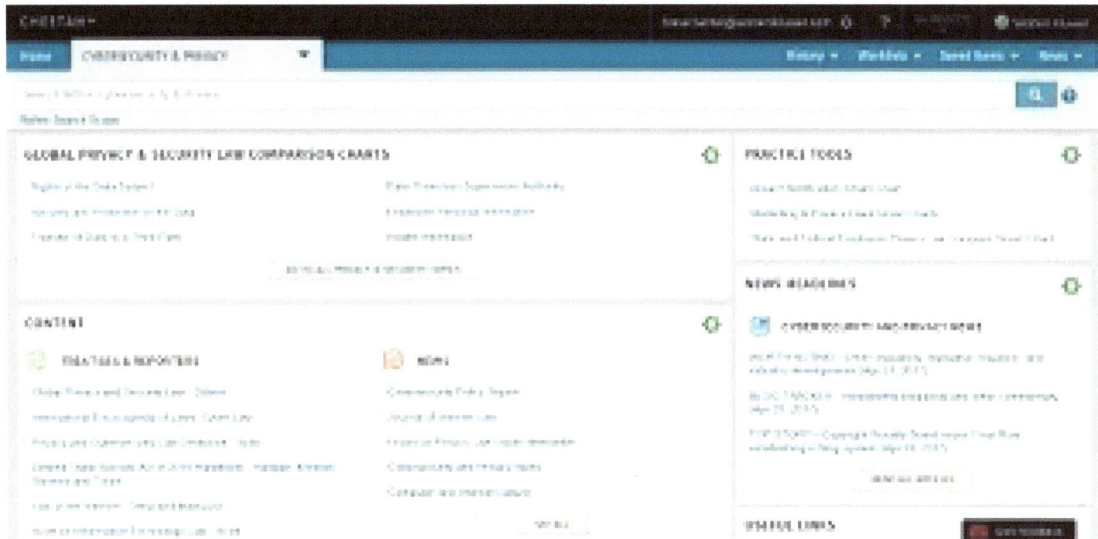

The new cyber security product offers access to international, federal, and state laws and regulations. The product is built on the Cheetah research platform. The very popular "Smart charts" allow lawyers to compare jurisdictional requirements and include expert commentary and procedural "know how." The Breach Notification Smart Chart is one of the most popular components of the product. International law comparison charts cover 66 countries enabling lawyers to select and compare the laws of multiple countries. "Useful links" provide direct access to important government agency websites. The Cybersecurity Policy Report a weekly newsletter tracks emerging policy developments. Expert guidance is available from 14 treatises and newsletters. Later this month they will be adding medical privacy statutes.

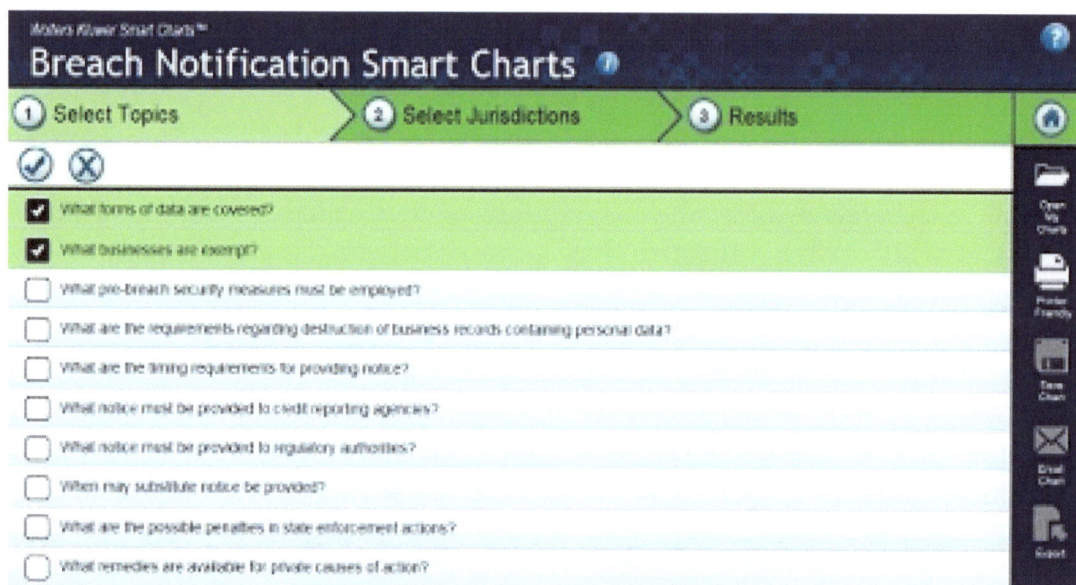

Wolters Kluwer's International Arbitration product is the leading international arbitration product. It was first published as a CD-ROM in 1998 and was launched as a digital product in 2003. After 14 years it was due for a makeover. Last week the publisher announced the launch of a re-designed platform. The new design relied heavily on user feedback to improve user experience and to streamline the research process.

Search enhancements include:

- Pre- and post-search filters
- Just did search terms
- Boolean enhanced with a flexible "near" command
- Results display with filter categories
- Search across multiple treatises
- Footnotes can be viewed as a "pop up" rather than an endnote

Wolters Kluwer's International Arbitration

The arbitration content has benefited from the publisher's recent implementation of a comprehensive content management system which enhances the ability to draw connections between a variety of content sets.

ktMine Apps

Wolters Kluwer also announced a new alliance with ktMINE, a provider of unique IP analytics. ktMINE subscribers can now access the ktMINE intellectual property analytics and documents on the Wolters Kluwer IP platform.

ktMINE includes four apps:

- Research
- Profiles of Companies
- Connectors
- Commercialization

ktMINE IP Platform

The All-in-One IP Research Platform

Search App
For broad landscape research

Profiles App
For Company research

Connections App
For understanding who is doing work around IP together

Commercialization App
Quickly find:
- Participants
- Value
- Deal terms
- Licensed patents

Wolters Kluwer | ktMINE

The product enables a researcher to locate companies associated with specific technologies. Content includes, analytics, royalty rates, licensees, SIC codes and links to full licensing agreements as well as recent IP news related to each company.

Ravel Launches Law Firm Analytics: Offers Law Firm Rankings, Competitive Intelligence, and Knowledge Management

MAY 24, 2017

Today Ravel is launching Law Firm Analytics which is putting them squarely into the competitive intelligence and law firm performance-based litigation rankings business.

Law Firm Analytics aggregates all of a firm's cases and offers tracking, searchability, and analysis by practice area, court, judge, time period, and motion. An associate can analyze their firm's winning cases and also access winning arguments. Firm Analytics also provides a new Ravel framework for integrating with firms' internal document management systems, and provides results which combine public and private content in a seamless research experience.

Firm Analytics provides rankings of firms across key variables including practice area, case volume, venue experience, and motion win rates. These leaderboards allow comparisons across substantive performance metrics, a significant innovation to traditional revenue and size rankings. As part of this launch, they are releasing rankings of the top five law firms across employment, securities, antitrust, administrative law, and bankruptcy (more below).

- Understand a firm's litigation history by case type, venue, motion win rate, and judge.
- Rank and compare firms by their case volume and motion win rate across 30+ practice areas and specific venues.
- Create custom comparisons and reports using an array of variables.

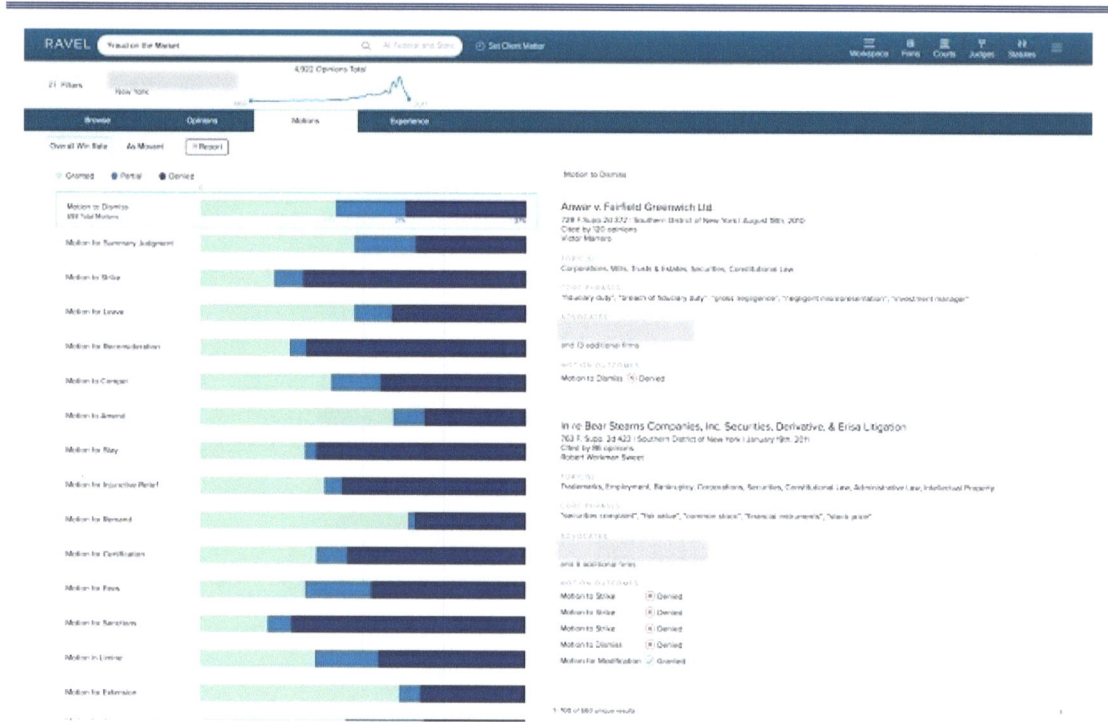

Figure 16: Ravel Law Firm Analytics

Knowledge Management: Lewis indicated that one ALM 100 law firm has integrated Ravel with documents from their DMS. This allows lawyers to simultaneously search both internal and external documents. They are now referring to this as a Knowledge Management Framework which they can develop as a custom solution for law firms.

Law Firms Love Rankings: Ravel Co-Founder Daniel Lewis points out that success rates in litigation are probably the better measure of a law firm value rather than profits per partner.

Rankings of Firms by Case Volumes Since 2014: Ravel's data is created by mining millions of federal and state cases, across 30+ practice areas and 400+ top U.S. firms. These rankings are based on activity since 2014.

Employment

Littler Mendelson
Jackson Lewis
Ogletree Deakins
Seyfarth Shaw
Morgan Lewis & Bockius

Securities

Robbins Geller Rudman & Dowd
Weil, Gotshal & Manges
Gibson Dunn
Paul, Weiss
Latham & Watkins

Antitrust

Jones Day
Kirkland & Ellis
Latham & Watkins
Skadden
Morgan Lewis & Bockius; Gibson Dunn (tied)

Administrative Law

Gibson Dunn
Perkins Coie
Arnold & Porter Kaye Scholer
Jones Day
Sidley Austin

Bankruptcy

Kirkland & Ellis
Locke Lord
Quinn Emanuel
Bryan Cave; Jones Day (tied)
Akin Gump

Treatises Are Not Dead, They Are Just Being Transformed: Lexis Launches First Video Practice Guide – Can the Gamified Treatise Be Far Behind?

MAY 24, 2017

Today LexisNexis is releasing a practice guide on federal civil practice, *The Wagstaffe Group Practice Guide: Federal Civil Procedure Before Trial* (http://www.lexisnexis.com/wagstaffe), that will be available in three formats: print, online in Lexis Advance, and eBook through LexisNexis Digital Library. This multimedia guide includes over 150 video clips of two to five minutes in length. This is the first video offering from a legal publishing market that I can recall since the release of Professor Robert Berring's *Commando Legal Research* series in 1989.

The LexisAdvance and Digital Library versions will be enhanced with video "mini lectures" by the author James M. Wagstaffe, former co-author of The Rutter Group's *Federal Civil Procedure Before Trial*. The press release describes the author as one of the country's preeminent First Amendment and defamation lawyers. Wagstaffe is also an adjunct professor in constitutional law and civil procedure at Hastings College of the Law and in Media Law at San Francisco State University and co-founder of Kerr & Wagstaffe LLP. The press release describes the videos as providing "rich, explanatory tips and practical insights... that enhance and complement the surrounding text in each chapter."

Sample Practice Tips/Strategic Points:

- Citizenship Rules for Diversity Strategic Tips for Plaintiff and Defendant Removal
- Analyzing Personal Jurisdiction – Objective and Strategy for Plaintiffs/ Defendants
- Analyzing Personal Jurisdiction – Strategic Points for Plaintiffs/ Defendants
- Motions to Dismiss Options and Strategies (entire section)

- Motions to Dismiss for Failure – Strategic Point — Plaintiff/Defendant to State Claim

According to Lexis this product will not compete directly with the iconic Moore's Federal Practice. Since this product is more focused on practice efficiency it appears to be positioned more in the LexisNexis Practice Advisor/Thomson Reuters Practical Law space.

Will Video Morph into Video Gaming?

Sean Fitzpatrick, Managing Director of North American Research Solutions at LexisNexis, quoted in the press release, describes how the product is positioned: "With its release and the addition of embedded video content directly within the legal research tools our customers use most, we're bringing practical guidance to life. Not only are we providing the smartest and most relevant content to the market, but we are doing so in a manner that addresses the changing needs of our customers."

I can't help but think that we already have a generation of lawyers whose hands itch for a game controller when they hear the word "video." I think it is time to think outside the traditional treatise. I assume that video is only the beginning. I could see gamification having a place in litigation strategy. As I always say, Lexis has bought so many amazing assets, I can't help but meditate on amazing mash-ups. Imagine Professor Wagstaffe illustrating a winning motion strategy and then enhancing it with an interactive, comparative outcome chart from Lex Machina.

Access: *The Wagstaffe Group Practice Guide: Federal Civil Procedure Before Trial* that will be available in three formats: print, online in Lexis Advance, and eBook, but will require a separate subscription.

Wolters Kluwer Leaps to the Head of the Class with "SmartTasks" Customizable Corporate Know-How and Offers a Free Federal Legislative Knowledge Center

MAY 31, 2017

Wolters Kluwer must be offering free double espresso shots every morning to their product developers and editors. Do they even sleep these days? Less than a month ago I wrote about the release of their Cybersecurity & Privacy platform, the relaunch of their International Arbitration platform, and their alliance with IP analytics provider ktMINE. Today they are announcing the release of "Corporate SmartTasks" which follows on their May 18th launch of a free Federal Regulatory Knowledge Center beta site.

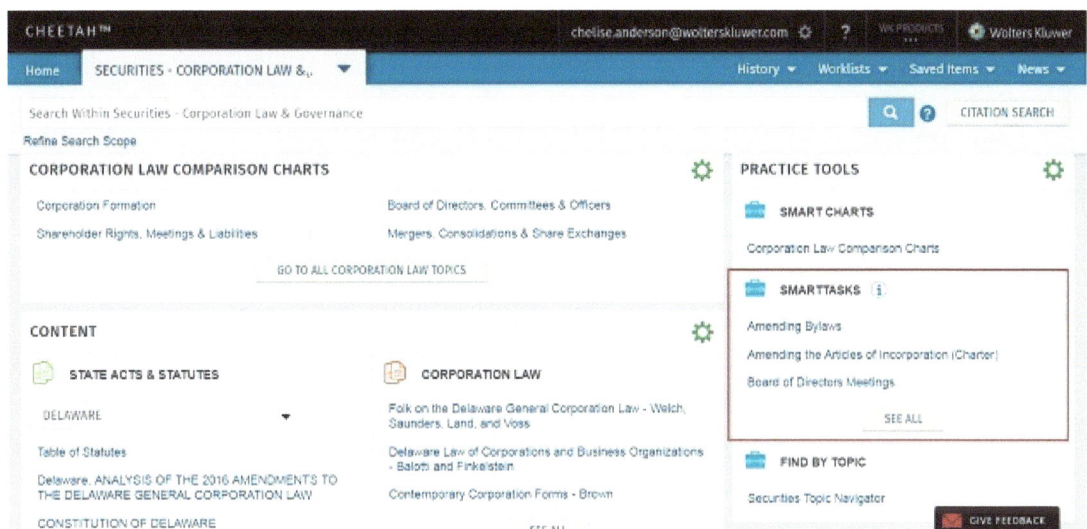

Figure 17: The Wolters Kluwer SmartTask Corporate Suite

SmartTask Corporate Suite – Already at the Head of the Class – Offers Firms Customizable Know How

The SmartTask Corporate Suite is positioned to pitch to the Practical Law, Lexis Practice Advisor audience by offering transactional workflow guidance with analysis. I will cut to the chase. They have already outdone the competition by allowing firms to customize the tasks and more importantly to add their own documents to the workflow. If there is one consistent criticism I have heard from partners when they see existing products, it is not wanting their associates to model cookie cutter documents. They ask: "How do we add our own documents?" It is a great question which I have been asking TR and LN repeatedly over the past few years. Every firm wants to believe they can add their own secret sauce... when they are ready to do so. The SmartTask platform will give them a leg up on a serious KM initiative which all too often can't get out of the gate. WK provides a template on which firms can build their own know how. Brilliant! They can't yet compete with Thomson Reuters or LexisNexis on breadth of content, but they could leapfrog into the lead by offering a lower cost and customizable alternative.

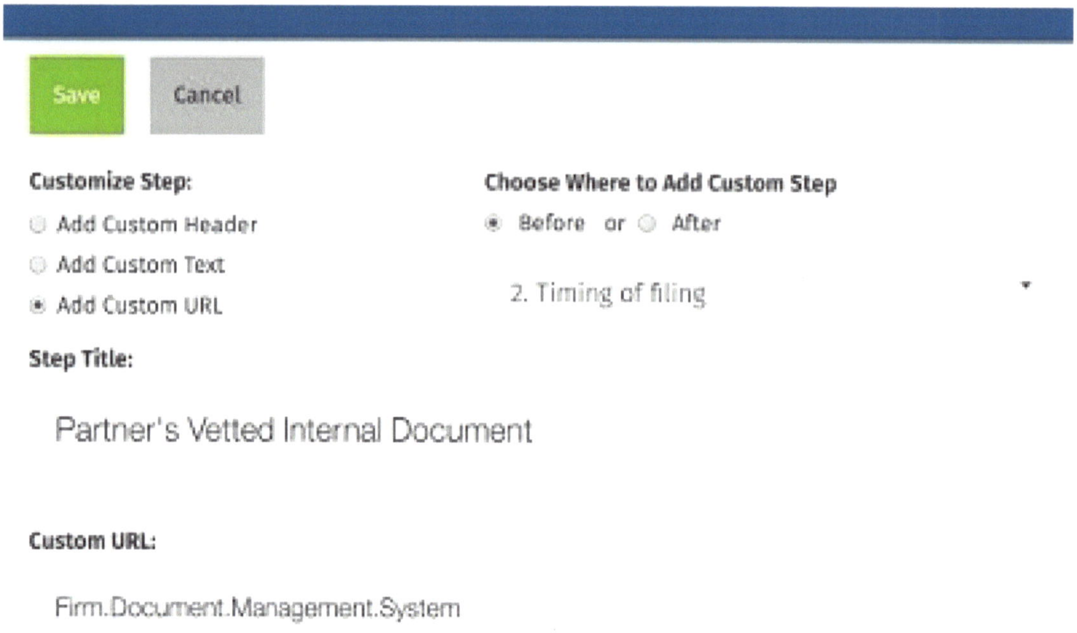

Save   Cancel

Customize Step: **Choose Where to Add Custom Step**

○ Add Custom Header   ◉ Before or ○ After

○ Add Custom Text

◉ Add Custom URL   2. Timing of filing

Step Title:

Partner's Vetted Internal Document

Custom URL:

Firm.Document.Management.System

Figure 18: Customizable Law Firm Content

SmartTask offers step by step guidance for standard transactional tasks such as amending bylaws, corporate formatting, drafting an SEC filing or choosing a form of business entity. The SmartTasks were designed with client demands for efficiency in mind. Dean Sonderegger, Vice President & General Manager of Legal Markets & Innovation, is quoted in their press release: "Attorneys are facing increased pressure to find new ways to make their practice more efficient... the SmartTask Corporate Suite provides a full set of resources, including workflow tools, which enables firms to standardize common legal practices, ensuring consistency and efficiency."

The benefits of SmartTask include:

- Practical Legal Guides – easy to follow, interactive, practical legal guides with practice notes and expert analysis
- Single Access Point – SmartTasks are integrated with direct links to pointed sections of laws and regulations, treatise materials, and primary sources
- Expert-created, step-by-step guides created by attorneys for attorneys

Unique features include:

- The ability to add your firm's own practice notes, in-house documents, or third-party content to any task
- The ability to standardize practices to help ensure consistency in attorney work product and increase realization rates

A complete list of SmartTask is listed available here: https://lrus.wolterskluwer.com/store/federal-developments-knowledge-center/

Free Access to the Federal Developments Knowledge Center Beta Site

I have now lived through six presidential election cycles since moving to D.C. in 1993. New Presidents and shifting Congressional majorities always generate uncertainty – this year is no different, though perhaps a bit more shrill. Wolters Kluwer is seizing the opportunity to balm the collective angst with data. They have launched a beta site for *The Federal Developments Knowledge Center*.

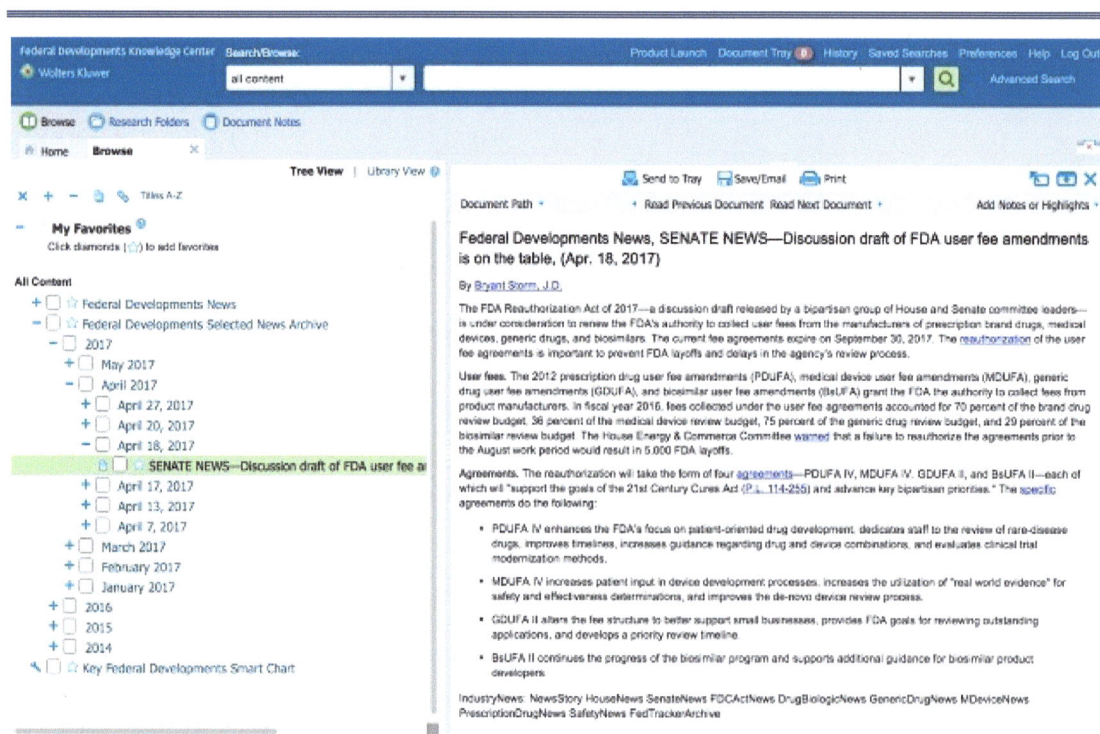

Figure 19: The Federal Developments Knowledge Center

Federal Developments Knowledge Center (FDKC) – currently in Beta – provides an easy to use site to survey the shifting legislative and regulatory landscape. Content includes:

- Daily updates of executive actions, legislative and regulatory developments
- Breaking news with rich analysis from Wolters Kluwer's attorney editors
- Enacted laws and final rules
- Impact analysis of executive orders, presidential memoranda, proposed legislation and regulations
- Key Developments SmartChart organized by practice area to track changes, provide current status and next steps, and offer insight on possible client impact.

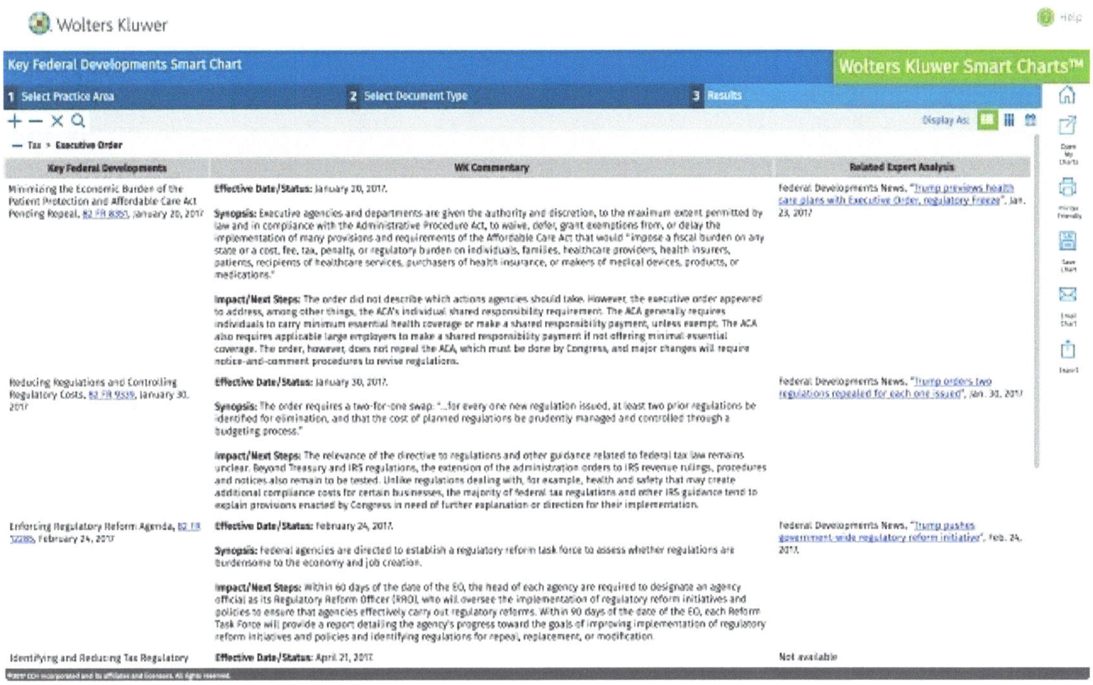

Figure 20: Federal Developments Smart Chart

The Beta period is expected to end in the summer. Additional content will be added which cover additional "hot topics" such as Global Trade, Environment, Energy, and Immigration. Perhaps most importantly they plan to add predictive analytics which will forecast the likelihood that legislation will be enacted.

Wolters Kluwer will update the platform with a system of scraping government websites and databases which will be enhanced with metadata to provide custom search filtering. A staff of over 100 writers and legal analysts will select and analyze the most important developments each day. The Federal Developments Knowledge Center will cover all federal agencies, all legislative actions, including those by congressional committees, and all executive actions. Wolters Kluwer editors will assess which actions are most likely to impact customers and their clients and provide a summary of the primary source document with a link to the primary source, as well as the potential impact and next steps toward enactment or implementation.

The Market Context

The Federal Knowledge Center is a logical development given Wolters Kluwer's deep expertise in the regulatory arena. The addition of predictive analytics is a smart way to introduce a practical AI application in a client advisory context. LexisNexis has already added predictive analytics for legislation on their legal research platform. Bloomberg BNA, which competes more directly with Wolters Kluwer in the regulatory space, has added predictive analytics for litigation but not for legislative or regulatory activity. Voxgov, which scrapes a wider variety of materials from federal websites, does not include any editorial analysis of legislation or regulation.

LexisNexis Acquires Ravel Law: A Tipping Point for Legal Analytics and the Second Wave of Legal KM

JUNE 9, 2017

Back in March I reported on a rumor that Ravel Law would be acquired by LexisNexis. Today LexisNexis and Ravel announced that Ravel Law is in fact being acquired by LexisNexis. Ravel Law was developed by Stamford Law grads Daniel Lewis and Nik Reed and offered a research platform which radically altered the way research results were delivered and displayed. They later offered a series of innovative analytics tools which provide insights into judicial precedential behavior, courts, motions, and law firm litigation trends. Since Lexis acquired another legal analytics company, Lex Machina in November 2015, I was curious to learn why LexisNexis decided to acquire another product offering legal analytics. Today I posed some questions to Ravel Law co-founder Daniel Lewis and LexisNexis VP of product management Jeff Pfeifer.

I tried to pin down Pfeifer and Lewis on the future of the Ravel Law product in the low cost legal research market. Pfeifer responded by confirming that LexisNexis would keep Ravel's commitment to provide public access to the Harvard Case law archive on the Ravel Law platform. The press release however refers to Lexis integrating Ravel technology and designating content as "powered by Ravel Law."

What's Next? The press release specifically indicates that Ravel content and/or technology will be integrated into these Lexis Analytics products:

- LexisNexis MedMal Navigator
- LexisNexis Verdict & Settlement Analyzer
- Intelligize

- Lex Machina
- Lexis Litigation Profile Suite

Ravel Law's data visualization tool and access to Harvard case law PDF images will enrich Lexis Advance.

Retaining the Ravel Team. Lewis and Reed, the co-founders of Ravel, have both been offered senior positions at LexisNexis and will report to Pfeifer. They will focus on creating new solutions for the legal market.

Ravel will remain in its current San Francisco location in order to retain their existing team which includes lawyers, data scientists, and design experts. This will also enable them to leverage the Silicon Valley talent pool. According to Lewis the acquisition should not be viewed as "Ravel having reached a finish line." To the contrary, he sees the Lexis acquisition as allowing the impact of Ravel technology to reach millions of lawyers through a larger platform.

According to Pfeifer, Lexis has made a $1 billion investment to re-architect the Lexis Advance platform and Lexis content. They will integrate Ravel's machine learning technologies while also developing new machine learning and AI applications.

When will the analytics tipping point occur?

I estimate that in five years legal analytics will become a core competency demanded by state bar associations – similar to the recent adoption of standards for technology competence in many states.

Lewis believes that introducing analytics in a more familiar application such as Lexis Advance will probably accelerate lawyers' understanding and embrace of analytics as a critical practice tool. Lewis hopes that the Lexis/Ravel integration will create a platform in which analytics will simply evolve into an intuitive dimension of case law research.

Driving the Second Wave of Knowledge Management

According to Pfeifer, Lexis is rapidly moving towards leveraging content from Intelligize (which was previously acquired) to deploy analytics and language analysis on law firm data for transactional documents. He sees a similar opportunity for leveraging the Ravel technology as well as other technology that Lexis is developing in house. Pfeiffer suggests that the legal market is about to witness a second wave of knowledge management. Lexis is in the process of creating tools which will enhance internal law firm data with machine learning tools. These new tools will enhance the documents and extract firm data and analytics which can be combined with external data and analytics. All three of Lexis' recent acquisitions: Intelligize, Lex Machina, and Ravel support a LexisNexis vision to enrich data and drive access to data analytics conclusions.

The Ravel Legacy. In the press release, Lewis cited the Harvard Law School alliance which provides open access to all U.S. case law: "We've digitized American law – a contribution to society that will outlive all of us."

Thoughts on Market Impact. Fastcase is the company which competed most directly with Ravel in offering a sophisticated research product to firms in search of a lower cost alternative to Lexis, Westlaw, and Bloomberg Law. I asked Ed Walters, CEO of Fastcase, if he had any thoughts to share on the Lexis/Ravel deal: "I can definitely see the fit. LexisNexis has been seeking an injection of entrepreneurship – Intelligize, LexMachina, and now Ravel – and Ravel gets to use the giant sandbox of data in LexisNexis. It's a validation of the importance of analytics in the next wave of legal research."

Bloomberg Law was the first of the major legal vendors to integrate comprehensive federal case law analytics for all types of litigation into their legal research desktop. (By contrast Lex Machina data is exposed in Lexis Advance for IP, Securities, and Antitrust cases only.) In addition, Bloomberg has added Compliance Rick Benchmarks and a Business Intelligence Center to their platform.

Thomson Reuters brought the first legal analytics product into the market over ten years ago. The Thomson Reuters Intelligence Center remains a stand-alone product which is used primarily by marketing and research teams in law firms. I reached out to Thomson Reuters today to determine if they are preparing to launch a legal analytics product which is integrated into the lawyer's desktop in order to compete more directly with LexisNexis and Bloomberg Law offerings. TR had no comment on their specific plans regarding analytics.

Here is the letter Ravel sent to their customers:

Dear Ravel Law Customer:

We are pleased to share that today LexisNexis announced its acquisition of Ravel Law, further extending our unparalleled capabilities in the analytics space. This exciting acquisition strengthens the LexisNexis position as the leader in legal analytics by expanding the LexisNexis Legal Analytics suite of products through full integration of Ravel judicial analytics, data visualization technology and exclusive case law PDF content from the Harvard Law Library into **Lexis Litigation Profile Suite®** and **Lexis Advance®**.

As a Ravel Law customer, I'd like to share a few details of how this acquisition will benefit you.

- **New and powerful capabilities in one platform.** Combining the resources of LexisNexis and Ravel Law will allow us to bring new innovations and additional content to Ravel customers.
- In early 2018, LexisNexis will integrate content and capabilities from Ravel Law with Lexis Advance, delivering new insights around judicial behavior that complement the product's current expert witness intelligence.
- Ravel Law's data visualization tool and access to Harvard case law PDF images will enrich the already expansive case law collection available on Lexis Advance.
- **Opportunity for unprecedented Insights.** The new expansive suite of analytics tools will provide unique opportunities for insight into judges and parties to cases. Lex Machina provides Legal Analytics about the behavior of judges, law firms, lawyers and parties, enabling lawyers to craft successful trial strategies, win cases and close business. Lexis Litigation Profile Suite, enhanced by Ravel Law technology, will complement this offering by providing insight into arguments that are likely to be persuasive to a judge. When combined with the behavior analysis from Lex Machina, litigators have the ability to build judge-specific arguments for use in court.
- **No changes to your current subscription.** For the immediate future, there are no changes to your Ravel Law subscription. You will continue to be billed and access the product as you always have.

As we move forward to leverage the many exciting opportunities this acquisition offers to our customers, we will make sure to share the details with you. For any additional questions, please contact your local Ravel Law representative.

Sincerely,

Sean Fitzpatrick, Managing Director, North American Research Solutions
Daniel Lewis, Chief Executive Officer, Ravel Law

Breaking News Exclusive: Fastcase Hires Seasoned Legal Publishing Exec — Launching New Strategy- Ready to Take on the Titans: Lexis, Westlaw, and Bloomberg BNA

JUNE 12, 2017

Fastcase is announcing today that a former LexisNexis executive, Steve Errick, will join the company's executive team as Chief Operating Officer. According to the press release, Errick will be "responsible for executing the company's strategic vision, developing new editorial products, and developing the company's organizational structure as the company expands."

Figure 21: Steve Errick

Errick's non-compete agreement with LexisNexis expires on June 30th and Errick will join Fastcase on July 1st. Errick most recently served as Vice President and Managing Director for Research Information for LexisNexis. In that role, he oversaw the Legal Research Information Product Division, with a $1 billion P&L portfolio. He led LexisNexis's development of workflow tools such as Lexis for Microsoft Office, E-book Digital Lending, Total Patent, and Litigation Suite which included MedMal Navigator. Errick also shepherded LexisNexis's acquisition of Law360, Securities Mosaic, and Sheshunoff/AS Pratt Financial Services.

Errick has an impressive resume with executive positions inside other legal publishing giants. He previously served as Vice President and General Manager of Wolters Kluwer's CCH Publishing division, as well as the Publisher of Thomson Reuters's Foundation Press division and Director of Acquisitions of Thomson's Clark Boardman Callaghan division.

The press release quotes Fastcase CEO Ed Walters: "We couldn't be more excited to have Steve join the team. Fastcase is an increasingly complex company, with sophisticated legal data updating operations, multiple product lines, and more than 100 employees in three offices – and we're growing all the time. Steve's deep relationships in the industry and his experience in managing legal publishing companies at scale will be important as we are growing into one of America's largest legal tech companies."

An Expanded Legal Publishing Strategy

Fastcase also announced that it would begin editorial publishing starting in 2018 to expand its offerings beyond primary law (case law, statutes, regulations, etc.). The company will launch its own imprint of treatises, secondary sources, and journals. It will also partner with bar associations in developing new state workflow products. This is a smart move, given relentless demand by clients for efficiency. Will they attempt to erode the market share of high ticket workflow tools offered by Thomson Reuters (Practice Point), LexisNexis (Lexis Practice Advisor), and Bloomberg BNA by offering a lower cost alternative?

Errick has worked in all facets of legal publishing so he is well positioned to navigate this expanded landscape. "Early in my career at West, my challenge was finding the best authors," Errick is quoted in the press release. "Most recently at LexisNexis it was acquiring the best companies and building a product team to drive those businesses. And now, I get this wonderful opportunity to use these diverse experiences to help accelerate the pace of the most innovative company in legal tech."

Fastcase President Phil Rosenthal elaborated on Errick's Fastcase portfolio which he describes as "developing the professional and management skills of the Fastcase team as it grows. Steve is a dynamic, hands-on leader who will help us build a world-class team and accelerate our growth. Everyone who has worked with Steve knows that he is very loyal to his teammates and helps them to be their best. Great teams win, and Steve is going to help us make a great Fastcase team even better."

Jumping the Chasm from Start-Up to Scale-Up

This Fastcase announcement comes just days after LexisNexis announced the acquisition of one of their key competitors, Ravel Law. In a phone conversation, Walters described how he and Rosenthal were determined to be one of the few legal tech startups to "jump the chasm," i.e., becoming a global enterprise player rather than an acquisition target. Fastcase hopes to follow the lead of companies like Google and Salesforce whose founders maintained independence long enough to become industry leaders.

While it may seem unlikely to some that Fastcase could ever displace the larger legal research systems, there are some factors which play in their favor. Unlike Lexis and Westlaw which are subsidiaries of huge global public companies, Fastcase is a private company which can call its own shots and perhaps move more quickly to adopt transformative, emerging technologies. Bloomerg BNA, which is also a private company, has faced low enterprise adoption rates due to its high price point in a legal market seeking to reduce the overhead costs of online research. Until now, Fastcase has positioned itself as a low-cost commodity research product focused on primary law. In the past year they acquired one of their competitors, Loislaw from Wolters Kluwer and last week competitor Ravel Law was acquired by LexisNexis, enabling Fastcase to solidify its dominance of the low-cost market. This strengthened market position combined with Errick's deep market expertise and a new strategy including an expanded product line of secondary sources and workflow tools should, at the very least, enable Fastcase to move "up market" while eroding some market share of the premium priced legal research platforms.

Lex Machina "DeCodes" Commercial Litigation: Launches Latest Analytics Insights into Business Torts and Contract Litigation

JUNE 20, 2017

Lex Machina

Owen Byrd, the Chief Evangelist at Lex Machina is really excited about the latest module of legal analytics. Byrd provided me with a preview of the new commercial litigation product. While he is proud of all the Lex Machina modules, he sees the commercial product as providing lawyers with a truly unique set of insights. According to him, until today there was no easy way to isolate analytics for the most common types of commercial litigation cases: "breach of contract" and "business tort." Sophisticated docket researchers have been frustrated by the gaps in the federal NOS codes which impair the tracking and analysis of many important types of litigation.

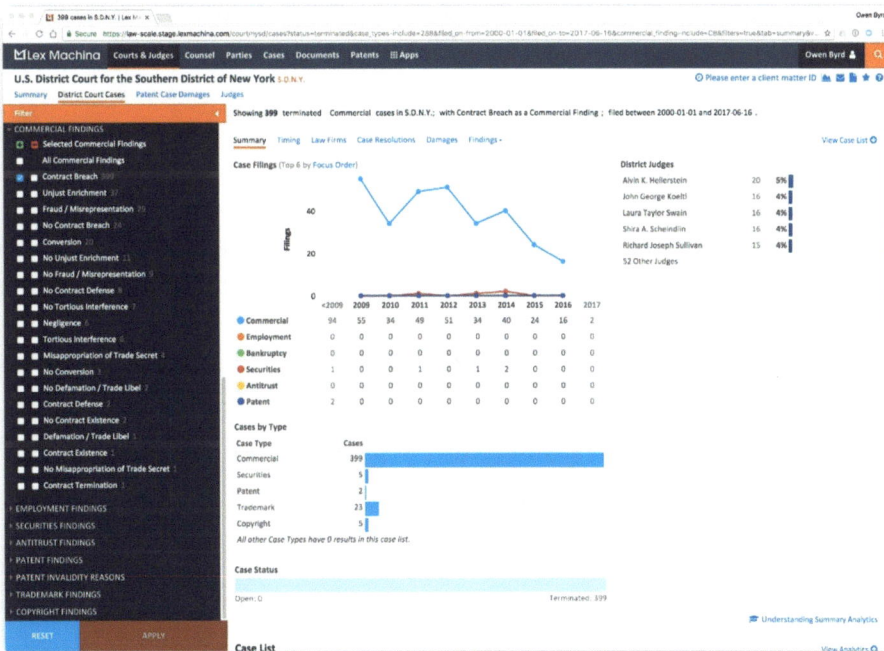

Engineering a "Nature of Suite" Code

The first question I asked Byrd was: "How did you go about identifying commercial cases?" After extensive interviews with commercial litigators, Lex Machina determined that Breach of Contract and Business Tort were the most important types of commercial litigation controversies. Using a combination of machine learning, natural language processing and human, attorney coders Lex Machina was able to create a "virtual NOS" code for this important subset of business litigation. This new set of cases required practice-specific tagging for issues such as contract breach, existence, rescission and termination as well as contract defense and unjust enrichment. Business tort findings include conversion, defamation/trade libel, and fraud.

According to the press release, of over 62,000 commercial cases filed since 2009, 80% include a breach of contract claim, and 57% include a business tort claim. PACER, the online platform containing federal docket entries and related documents, does not contain a Nature of Suit (NOS) code that captures all commercial cases. Lex Machina's new offering resolves the challenge of defining "commercial" cases, which are often filed under multiple NOS and Cause of Action (COA) codes. Approximately 25% of commercial cases meet the definition of an intellectual property, securities, or antitrust case, and are coded in PACER as such. Commercial litigation generated $6 billion in billings for U.S. law firms annually.

New Lex Machina features include:

- **Expanded case timing analytics:** In addition to time to dismissal, trial, and termination, Lex Machina has added time to permanent injunction and summary judgment.
- **New damages categories:** Commercial cases include contract damages, restitution, and other damages, as well as tort compensatory damages and punitive damages.
- **New breach of contract and business tort findings:** New tags have been added for contract breach, existence, rescission, and termination, as well as contract defense and unjust enrichment. Business tort findings include conversion, defamation/trade libel and fraud.

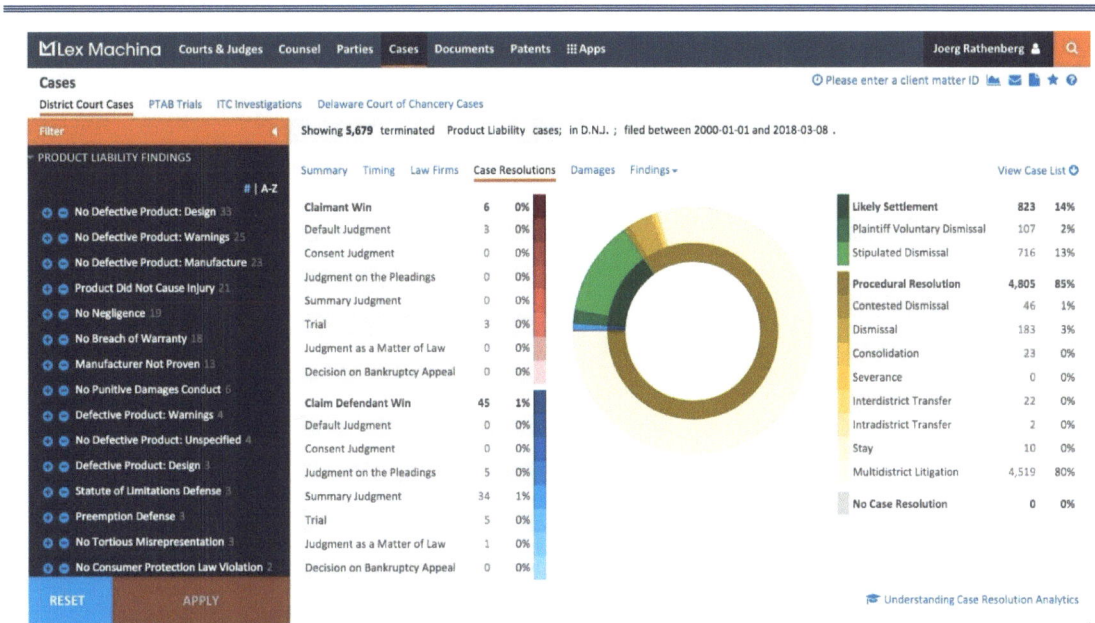

Hats off to the Lex Machina team. The new commercial module is an important achievement in leveraging technologies such as machine learning and natural language processing to identify, code, and expose important new subsets of litigation which have been buried in the arcane coding of federal PACER system. According to Byrd, Lex Machina plans to release additional modules through the end of the year, including employment law, products liability, and commercial bankruptcy.

Guess Who's Coming to AALL?: New Exhibitors Part 1: Litigation, Corporate and IP Vendors

June 21, 2017

The AALL Conference Exhibit Hall gives attendees the chance to take a long and winding stroll through aisles lined with vendors promoting the latest innovations and offering a "first look" at new products. It is a festival of food, swag, and serendipitous encounters with old colleagues as well as the chance to meet new ones. I especially value the opportunity for a one-on-one engagement with vendors and a quick tutorial on a hot new product. Since the major legal vendors dominate the Exhibit Hall at AALL, it is easy to overlook first-time vendors with unfamiliar names and unknown products.

I thought it would be interesting to take a peek at the twelve new exhibitors at the 2017 Conference and provide some insights into their products. This post will be written in two parts. Part one focuses on vendors offering products for litigation, corporate and IP Practice needs. I recommend taking a close look at each of these vendors. Even though you may have a product which covers the same legal issues, you are likely to discover that each of these vendors is offering a unique type of service or analysis of an old problem. Many are offering AI-driven and custom solutions. Stop by and welcome these new exhibitors to the AALL exhibit call in Austin.

For a complete list of exhibitors, visit

http://iebms.heiexpo.com/iebms/oep/oep_p1_exhibitors.aspx?oc=13&ct=OEP &eventid=5027

I have only used the products of two of these new vendors: Casetext and voxgov (which will be covered in Part 2 of this post). Information for the remaining vendors is taken from their websites.

In what may be a first, the AALL "New Product of the Year" award went to a startup Casetext CARA – a feat all the more remarkable since they had no official presence at AALL in 2016. Last year many attendees including myself met Pablo Arredondo, who was walking the halls and providing on-the-fly demos.

I asked Jake Heller, President of Casetext, why he thought it was important to exhibit at AALL. "Law librarians are the world's true experts in all things legal research and they have been an integral part of CARA's development and deployment. Particularly considering CARA being honored as new product of the year, we thought this was a great time to launch our inaugural AALL booth. We look forward to seeing everyone there!"

Casetext which offers free case law research, access to analytical memos from 150 law firms, and a crowd sourced citator called "We-cite" is launching their first "fee based" product: CARA. Casetext currently includes over 7 million primary documents including case law from all 50 states. CARA stands for Case Analysis Research Assistant. CARA is very easy to use. All a lawyer has to do is drag and drop a brief into CARA. Instead of searching with keywords, CARA uses the entire brief as the query. CARA data-mines the brief by extracting both the text and the citations from the document. The CARA analysis looks at direct relationships and "implied" relationships between the cited cases in the brief and related opinions in the Casetext database. CARA uses latent semantic analysis to sort the results. The CARA results report includes a list of "suggested cases" and a CARA-generated analysis of those cases.

Dispute Resolution Data enables you to discover the value of arbitration and mediation through the exploration of aggregated international case data.

Aggregated dispute resolution data will provide professionals in the field with insight through historic and current geographic and case-type reports on dispute resolution claims, durations, and processes. This information is valuable in assessing risk management and strategy.

focusedIP is the first to provide patent practitioners with a high-quality Patent Trial and Appeal Board (PTAB) decision database accessible by state-of-the-art search tools and data analytics. focusedIP is the only vendor that has generated a complete, accurate, and reliable PTAB decision database. We have taken the time to ensure that our database accurately represents the complete body of published PTAB decisions – including the 100,000+ plus PTAB Appeals, and not just the 2600+ AIA Trial Decisions.

GDE MEXICO LEGAL LLC

www.nafta-law.com

"Through timely and proactive solutions we help your international ventures proceed efficiently and with minimal legal cost. We provide you with valuable information and develop practical tools to ensure you make the best business decisions."

MYLOGIQ

MyLogIQ uses AI to analyze filings for public companies. Welcome to the 21st century. Data Blending with MyLogIQ's AI Powered Integrated Platform.

CIQ-CompanyIQ™ is a single integrated platform of multiple domains of information, which covers ALL public companies. It provides a comprehensive 360-degree profile of companies delivered in real time. Our solution will help you cut costs and increase efficiency.

With CIQ-Company IQ™ you can perform concept-based searches and quickly identify changes between documents. You can also pinpoint relevant peer or industry disclosures for any concept and access *six* other domains of information, not covered by other data providers.

Our CIQ-Company IQ™ cloud-based software is the most robust research tool in the industry. We provide a 360-degree compliance perspective for all public companies.

PERCEPTION
PARTNERS

Perception partners describes three different types of services on their website. 1) Intell competitive monitoring, mines the deep web for innovation opportunities, and IP risk, 2) IP search, and 3) Monitor for counterfeits, brand protection services produce evidence of infringement to support takedown requests, and technology landscaping offers expert to map out IP strategy.

Social Media Information

Social Media Information is a managed service provider whose mission is to locate, investigate, and preserve human information from social media and the web. "Our proprietary technology and team of in-house analysts allow us to produce actionable human intelligence reports and preserve web evidence efficiently and with a high degree of accuracy."

This year's conference will be held at The Austin Convention Center, July 15th to 18th in Austin, Texas.

Guess Who's Coming to AALL? Part 2: Government Information and Workflow Tools

JUNE 25, 2017

Yesterday's post highlighted seven vendors which will be first-time exhibitors at AALL in Austin next month.

Those vendors offer tools which are primarily targeted at litigation, corporate, and Intellectual Property practices. Today's five vendors are more diverse. Several offer a wide range of services which fall broadly within "workflow improvement." Voxgov is the only vendor in today's group which focuses purely on providing a unique set of content on a research platform. I asked voxgov founder Robert Dessau why he had decided to exhibit at AALL this year. "With expertise in the collection and management of a broad range of original source material from Federal and State governments we view AALL as the ideal environment in which to introduce our newest addition, voxgov Energy, designed specifically for the legal market. We look forward to assisting, collaborating with, and incentivizing those who need visibility into who in government is saying what on any energy-related issue at any time. Visitors to our booth will have the chance to win a free one-year subscription to voxgov Energy. Look forward to meeting you Austin."

Beyond the obvious Statutes-at-large and CFR, voxgov scrapes over 9,000 U.S. government URLs, including social media, and has created a massive database which can be searched and analyzed for trends by agency, issue, and political party. The government information lawyers normally rely upon such as statutes and regulations only represents about 10% of the voxgov database. The vast majority of government materials in voxgov are collected from over 14,000 government websites. The document types include: Press Releases, News, Notices, Columns, Articles, Op-Eds, Decisions, Opinions, Orders, Events, Media Advisories, Fact Sheets, Newsletters, Bulletins, Recalls, Alerts, Reports, Publications, Speeches, Statements, Remarks, Testimony, and Transcripts, along with Social Media from official government sources, Twitter, Facebook, You Tube and more. Voxgov only collects information authored or adopted by the U.S. Federal Government and published on official government websites. All of the data is enriched with extensive metadata which supports sophisticated filtering and trending.

Their website states that Casebriefs offers "the most widely used supplements for higher education and newly minted professionals."

Although they offer resources for a wide range of professionals there is plenty of content for law students including, Casebriefs, outlines, exam prep, and video lectures.

InfoTrack offers a wide range of services including interactive forms for electronic filing of government forms, an electronic signature tool called "SignIT," court document retrieval, and corporate services including corporate formation and entity searching. They also have a data visualization tool called "REVEAL" which charts entity relationships.

Powernote has an intriguing tagline: "Organize your internet."

They promote their product as "the only tool designed for the academic research process." But after looking at the website, I think this product has a broader audience including the law firm. government, and judicial markets. The product offers highlighting, categorizing and note-taking on any website. The product organizes research into an outline form. It also saves the URL links for all the sources in the outline. Frankly, it sounds like a great tool for any researcher no matter what their environment.

Sabinet offers a wide range of innovative library services including collaborative cataloguing, inter-library lending, and end-to-end library management systems.

They also offer support for digitization and information management projects, news monitoring, and access to journals.

Lexis Answers: Artificial Intelligence Without the Hyperbole; No Robot Lawyers in Sight – A Fastrack to Legal Answers

JUNE 26, 2017

LexisNexis

Entering the "no hyperbole" zone. No robots in sight.

I spent almost an hour last Friday talking to Jeff Pfeifer, Vice President of Product Management at LexisNexis, about the upcoming release of a new artificial intelligence enabled Lexis Advance feature called Lexis Answers. Instead of the "robot lawyer" hyperbole that has characterized many recent AI product announcements, Pfeifer (while enthusiastic for Lexis Answers) is refreshingly restrained in discussing the product. Most importantly he does not oversimplify the true complexity of legal research when applying AI to a specific set of facts. He describes Lexis Answers as getting lawyers to a "well informed starting point," speeding up basic research so lawyers can start more complex research. He sees Lexis Answers as the "next evolutionary step in a journey with big data sets which is moving towards human like interactions with machines using standard Dialog."

"Lexis Answers represents a paradigm shift in legal research. By delivering specific and actionable answers at the top of their search results, we're saving users effort previously spent analyzing pages of search results and legal documents—enhancing their workflow and empowering them to get more done in less time," said Sean Fitzpatrick, Managing Director of North American Research Solutions at LexisNexis.

The Answer Card

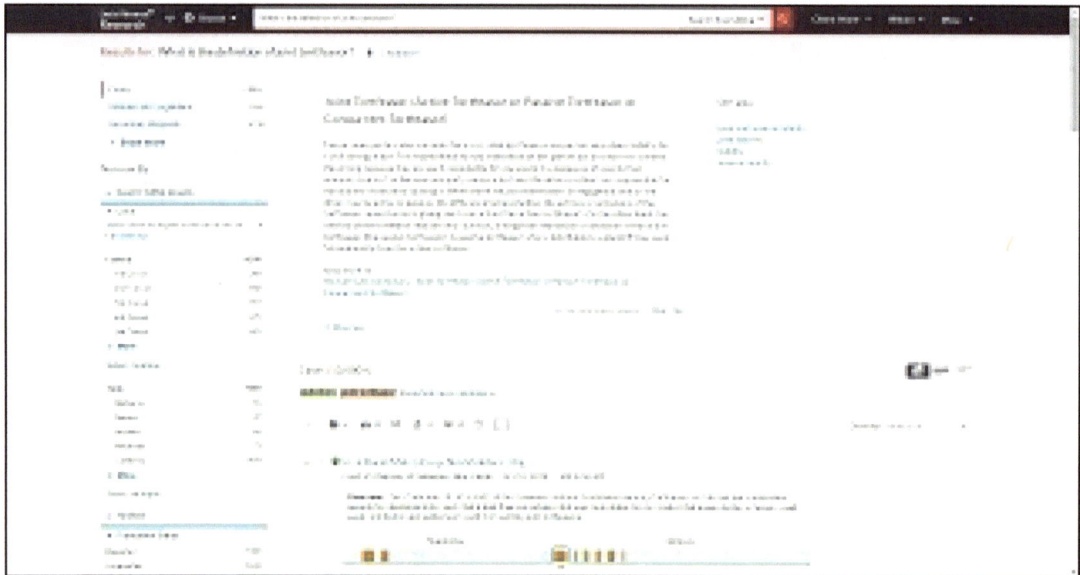

According to Pfeifer: "With Lexis Answers, our goal is to create a smarter staring point to legal research." When a lawyer types in a natural language question they see "The Answer Card" which displays four key things:

1. A concise answer – a starting point to smarter legal research
2. The authority for the answer, including case reference and date of the authority
3. Related legal topics that should be reviewed for complete and thorough research
4. A feedback feature – Was this information useful – Yes or No – that helps LexisNexis train our machine learning algorithms based upon user assessment of answer quality.

"Additionally, the result list is specially compiled based upon our analysis of the user's query and our interpretation of the user's query intent. The result list is uniquely curated to emphasize additional authority that is relevant to the user's question."

Types of Questions

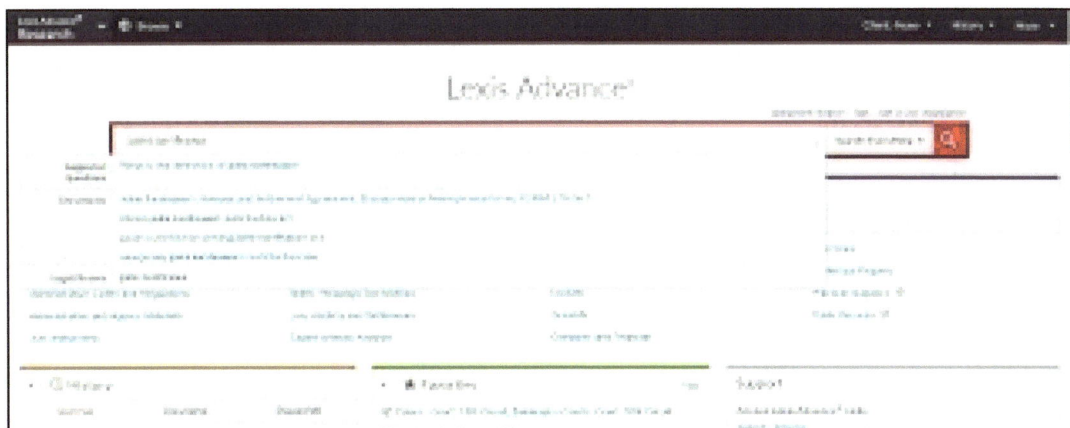

At this time Lexis Answers can provide answers for five types of legal questions:

1. Definitions
2. Elements
3. Standards of review
4. Legal doctrine
5. Burden of proof

According to Pfeifer, there are plans to "expand the collection of questions that are supported, and mine additional content types as we further build out our machine learning system."

Under the Hood

Lexis Answers has been in development at Lexis' Raleigh Tech Center for more than two years. The Raleigh center was established in 2015 as a "cognitive computing center of excellence." The Lexis Answers questions were informed by anonymized user logs. Specifically they looked at user queries that included input errors such as a really bad query syntax or partial questions that were not fully articulated.

Jeff summed it up as, "We have been sending the natural language processor to law school." Several years ago I wrote that the problem with the current state of legal AI was that so far machines could only respond and couldn't "Ask" questions to help researchers refine and clarify what they need. I am happy to see that LexisNexis is moving toward the research dialog.

Such is suggesting that the user limit by jurisdiction. They also anticipate voice iteration using clarifying questions to help the user.

I asked Pfeiffer if IBM's Watson technology was part of the solution, and he indicated that it was not. LexisNexis had internal knowledge which they combined with a variety of open source AI and machine learning technologies as well as programs available from Google and Amazon. These various pieces of technology were customized to meet the requirements of legal research. "The main goal was to provide immediate utility for standard case law researchers." Lexis Answers will be available to all subscribers at no additional cost.

Additional Features to Come – "Ravel Answers"

Although the LexisNexis acquisition of Ravel Law was only announced two weeks ago, they are already exploring how Ravel's technology can help them extend Lexis Answers. Pfeifer anticipates that the Ravel technology should allow them to extract phrases and legal expressions and enable them to add new kinds of questions and answers. In the future, they hope to be able to answer questions about judges, experts, and provide various kinds of profiles.

They will provide post-search filters so users can limit by jurisdiction in the near future. The only concern I see is that there could be a "legislative gap." It is not clear to me how a major legislative change which modifies or nullifies case law precedent can be reflected in machine learning results "overnight." For example, if there were sweeping tax reform which they changed the statute of limitation for tax fraud, it is not clear to me how this change would be immediately reflected in the results. Pfeifer indicated that they are well aware of this issue and are using the Lexis Shepherd's statutory analytics to identify changes in statutes.

When asked if Lexis Answers will be available on any non-English platforms, "At this time no," but Pfeiffer assured me that the technology they have built will be extensible to non-English platforms.

No Robot Lawyers, Just More Efficient Lawyers

Pfeiffer does not make overblown promises that this technology will eliminate associates. He talks like a man with a deep appreciation for the complexities and idiosyncrasies of how law would apply to a set of facts. In fact, he stated that there is rarely a question where the first response from Lexis Answers is the end of the legal research process.

The Competition

Thomson Reuters released a similar feature called Westlaw Answers in January 2016. However, that feature covered mostly state answers. Lexis Answers covers Federal and State case law answers. I am not aware of Bloomberg Law offering a similar feature – they only added "natural language" query feature earlier this year and had previously required Boolean queries. Wolters Kluwer has a Google plug-in for their Tax product which enables researchers to enter a natural language query and get an answer. Ross Intelligence also provides a natural language response to queries – though their product was limited to bankruptcy law and may recently have expanded to cover Intellectual Property.

Starting Today at No Additional Cost to Subscribers

At noon on June 26, 2017, LexisNexis will start turning on Lexis Answers for each of their accounts. Apparently, this has to be done on a client by client basis and they expect the entire process to be completed by the end of Tuesday, January 27.

The American Lawyer Highlights Rise of the CKO in 2017 Survey of Library, Knowledge Management, and Research Professionals

JULY 2, 2017

Last year I pleaded with ALM to change the name of their annual Library Survey since they had been predicting the end of libraries for about 14 years. It was time to stipulate that print collections are shrinking and move on to exploring the dynamic organizations which have emerged in their place.

This year *The American Lawyer* has finally renamed the annual survey as the "Survey of Law Firm Management Library and Research Professionals." The accompanying articles have shifted gear as well. The articles are titled "Law Librarian? Trying Chief Knowledge Officer" by Mary Ellen Egan (http://www.americanlawyer.com/id=1202791116149/Law-Librarian-Try-Chief-Knowledge-Officer), and "From Providing Data to Providing Insight," by Lizzy McLellan (http://www.americanlawyer.com/id=1202791117753/From-Providing-Data-to-Providing-Insight).

The first article focuses on the morphing of librarians into knowledge management professionals who are focused on evaluating and introducing tools which provide new kinds of insights for business and legal strategy, as well as competitive intelligence insights which are central to law firm strategies for success. The survey indicates that these intelligence responsibilities also include lateral candidate due diligence, research assisting with RFP responses, participating in client satisfaction research, and pricing projects. It should not be surprising that with these expanded roles, the survey reveals that law firms are willing to pay higher salaries.

Thought leaders in law firm knowledge management who are quoted in the article include: Greg Lambert, CKO at Jackson Walker; Marlene Gebauer, Director of Knowledge Solutions at Greenberg Traurig; Steve Lastres, Director of Knowledge Management Services at Debevoise and Plimpton; Catherine Monte, CKO at Fox Rothschild; Elizabeth Chappieri, CKO at Nixon Peabody; and Lucy Dylan, CKO at Reed Smith.

Lastres and Monte both highlight the challenge keeping up with the complex ecosystem of emerging tools offering AI and analytics. New products can offer law firms real competitive advantage but there are so many new startups with interesting ideas, it takes time to sort through the offerings and carefully assess the business case for each tool. Lastres explains the challenge: "We are on the front line of technological adoption. We have to evaluate each product and make recommendations to our attorney." The challenge is made all the more daunting by the universal imperative to contain costs.

Can Firms Afford Not to Have a CKO?

Chiapperi and Dillon highlight the transformation of the information professional's role. According to Nixon Peabody's Chiapperi, "Our role has evolved from providing data to really providing insight. You have to understand the business and understand what's going on in the industry." Dillon suggests that law firms without a CKO will be at a disadvantage. "It's important to have someone who is responsible for knowledge at the table with all the Chiefs to manage other functions... If it [knowledge] was lower down in the hierarchy of the organization we wouldn't benefit from all those synergies."

While Lexis and Westlaw still dominate digital budgets, Bloomberg and Wolters Kluwer still represent an important share of spending for knowledge resources. I could not help but note in the full statistical report how large the "other" categories were. Questions asking responders to identify other tools ranged from 30 to 60% of the resources identified. The full ALM intelligence report includes a detailed list of important resources that are gradually being adopted for competitive intelligence and analytics insights. I would like to suggest that ALM incorporate these products by name into next year's survey.

ROI Rules. Another important insight from the survey is the wide adoption of tools to manage digital resources. 78% of responders now use some tool to measure the utilization and calculate the ROI for each resource. As new tools emerge knowledge professionals have leveraged tools such as Research Monitor and Onelog to help them actively manage their portfolios of digital resources. These tools provide custom law firm analytics and insight to justify the cancellation of an under-performing product in order to introduce a more innovative and powerful new resource. That resource in turn will have to demonstrate rapid adoption in order to survive ROI analysis to make it into the next year's budget.

Understanding the Data. Thanks to ALM for relinquishing the print-centric survey and highlighting the important new roles played by information professionals. These are what I would describe as some "transition pains." The change in billable hours changed so dramatically that one has to assume there may have been a dramatic change in the number or responders or the size of the firms responding. The data regarding the volume of research requests handled is so variable that there may be a misunderstanding of the question by some of the responders. The Egan article highlights staffing ratios as a percentage? I could not find staffing or budget ratios in the full report at all.

ALM Intelligence will be hosting a breakfast presentation to discuss the results of the ALM survey at the upcoming AALL conference in Austin on July 16 at 7:30 A.M. at the Hilton Governor's Ballroom Salon B.

Bloomberg Law Relaunches Corporate Practice Center with In-House Counsel Focus: Compliance, Toolkits and Analytics

JULY 10, 2017

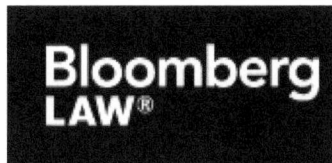

As market power shifts from law firms to in-house counsel, Bloomberg Law has responded by bulking up the Corporate Practice Center with resources designed to address the special needs of Chief Legal Officers, Chief Compliance Officers, and Chief Operating Officers. Earlier this year Bloomberg Law relaunched the Corporate Practice Center with materials developed with extensive input from corporate counsel at major U.S. companies. The Corporate Practice Center includes practice pages covering: compliance, legal operations, corporate governance, alternative business structures, litigation, and corporate news. In addition, an "In Focus, hot topics" section offers deep coverage of special topics such as proxy regulation and FCPA.

Bloomberg and the Association for Corporate Counsel (ACC) also announced that they had entered a strategic collaboration for Bloomberg Law to offer sponsored content, practice tools, and editorial expertise to ACC members through professional enrichment, educational, and development programs.

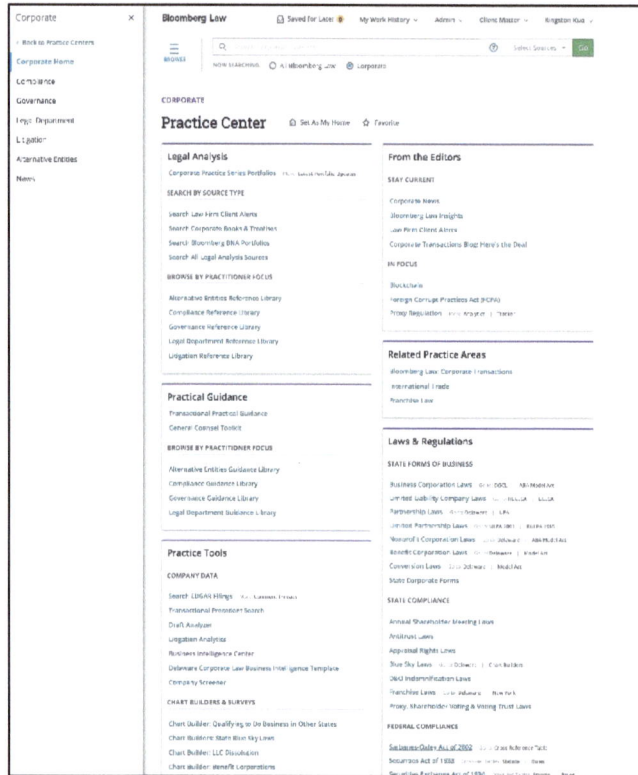

Figure 22: Bloomberg Law Corporate Practice Center

The Corporate Compliance Practice Page provides practical guidance. Sections focus on Risk Assessment & Benchmarking, Codes of Conduct, The Role of Management, Chief Compliance Officer & Board, and Due Diligence. The main focus of this practice page is ethics and compliance. The Bloomberg Law press release reports that according to the Association of Corporate Counsel Chief Legal Officers 2017 Survey, 74% of respondents rated ethics and compliance as the top challenge. In response, Corporate Practice Center features a multitude of practical guidance materials including overviews, checklists, annotated forms, model documents, and comparison surveys developed by attorneys at major U.S. corporations. It incorporates compliance content developed by the in-house legal department at U.S. Steel Corporation which provides users with step by step guidance for maintaining a corporate compliance program. The corporate practice center also includes sample form agreements and policies for routine tasks facing in-house attorneys.

The full Press Release is available at: https://www.multivu.com/players/English/8062531-bloomberg-law/

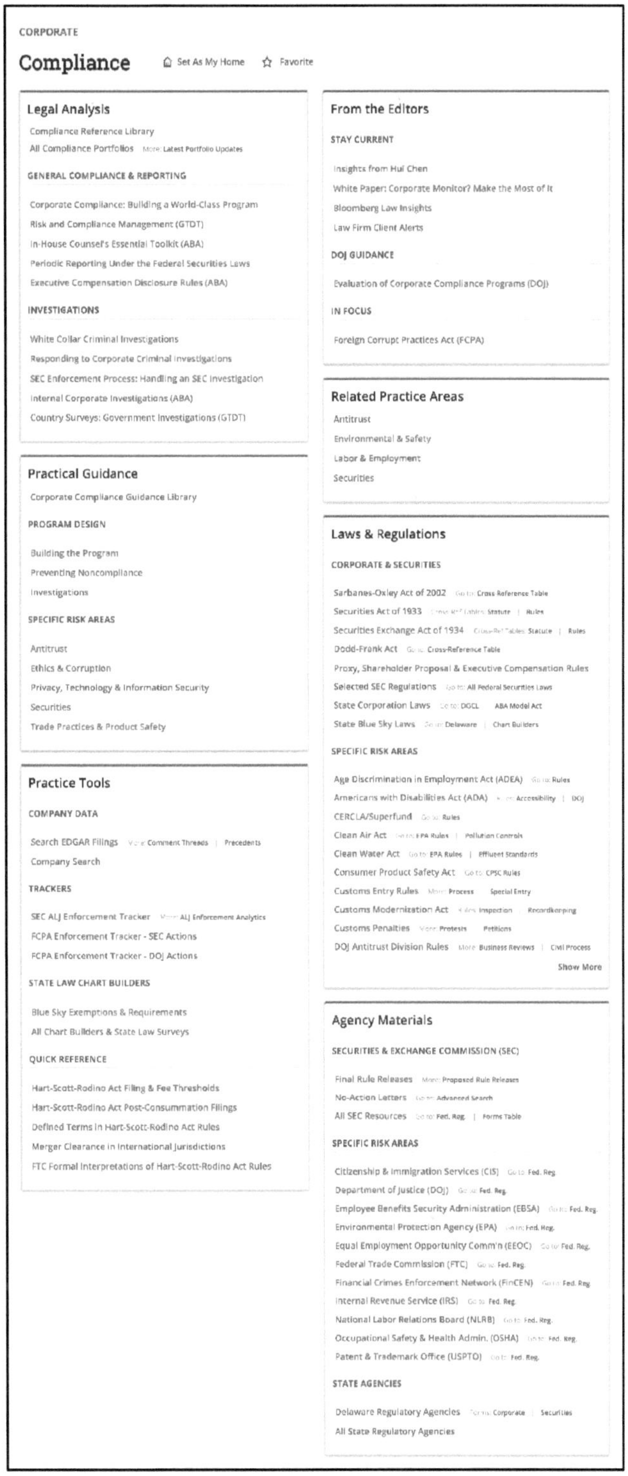

Figure 23: Bloomberg Law Compliance Practice Page

The Legal Department Practice Page was designed for General Counsel, Chief Legal Officers, and Chief Operating Officers. Content includes practical guidance on issues such as department structure, budgeting, operations, as well as specialized topics such as whistle-blowing and privilege. Special features include a Foreign Corrupt Practices Tracker, company profiles, agency filings, and primary source statutes.

The General Counsel Toolkit include agreements & policies, practical guidance, and legal analysis.

The Governance Practice Page provides a governance reference library, governance portfolios, State and Federal laws and regulations, precedent documents for incorporation, bylaws, audit committees, and other standard materials.

The Alternative Entities Practice Page covers, S Corporations, LLCs, Partnerships, and Limited Partnerships. Content includes legal analysis, guidance, precedents, laws, and regulations.

The Litigation Page offers a variety of trackers covering Delaware Chancery, U.S. Supreme Court, SEC Enforcement, FCPA, and Securities Enforcement. Other content includes dockets, agency material, and legal analysis.

In Focus and Analytics provides deep insights into an important practice issue such as "Investor Activism" which provides analytics for "proxy season" highlighting the sectors being targeted. We have seen a lot of products offering litigation analytics, but it is refreshing to finally see some slick corporate analytics.

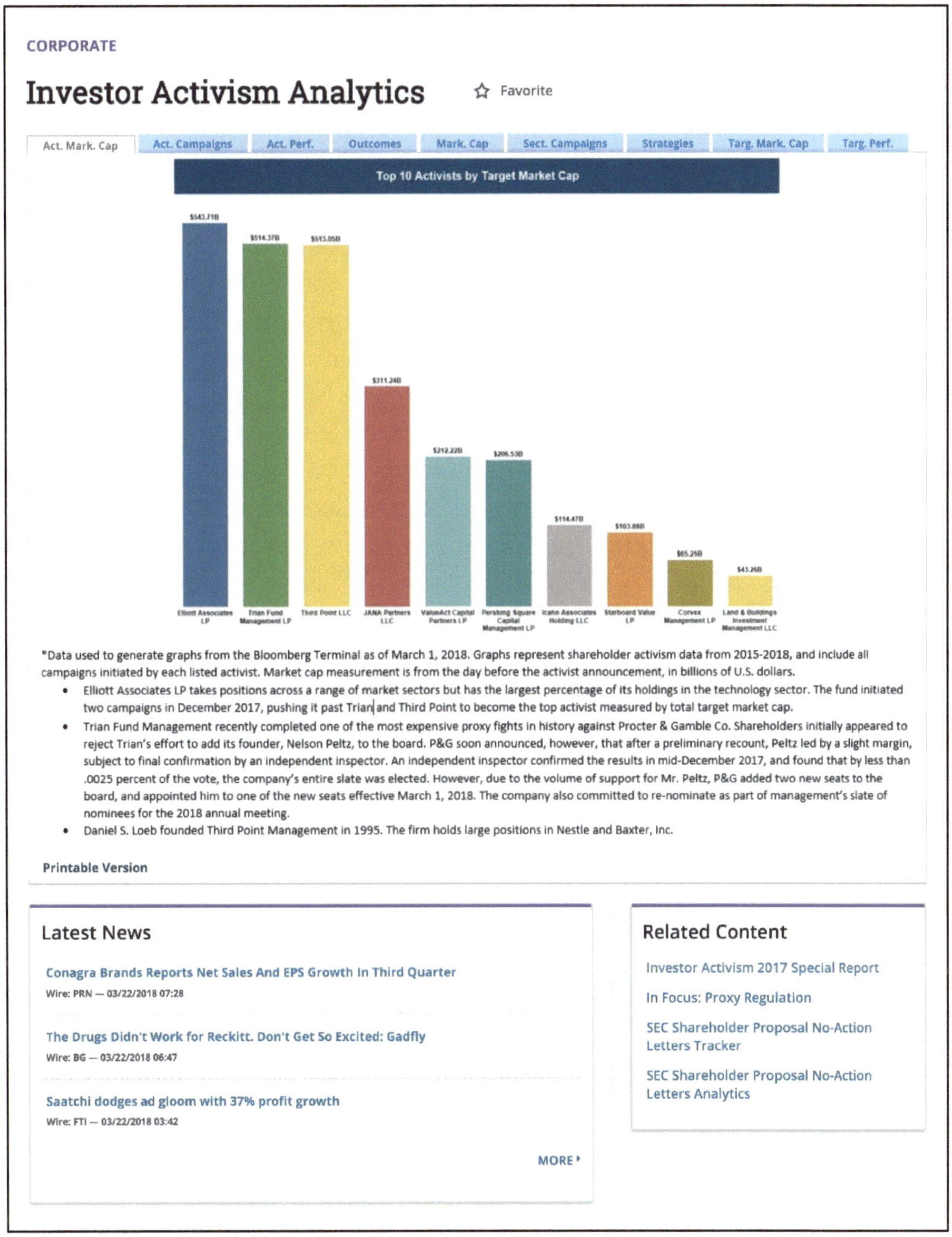

Figure 24: Bloomberg Law Proxy Season Analytics

Although the Corporate Practice Center was designed for in-house counsel, the content is available to all Bloomberg Law subscribers and will have obvious appeal to outside counsel in supporting the needs of their corporate clients.

The competition. Clearly these new enhancements are designed to enable Bloomberg Law to compete with Thomson Reuters Practical Law/Practice Point, and LexisNexis products Practice Adviser and Intelligize. Wolters Kluwer also recently entered this workflow enhancement space with a series of corporate workflow solutions branded as "SmartTasks." The past five years has seen a continuous expansion of workflow and artificial intelligence tools for lawyers. The value of current AI tools remains somewhat speculative, while workflow tools offer more immediate benefits to both junior and more senior lawyers who are continually pressed to maximize efficiency. Ironically, BNA (before being purchased by Bloomberg) deserves the credit for creating the first practical guidance resources for corporate lawyers. The BNA Corporate Practice Portfolios beat TR's Practical Law to the U.S. market by about a decade. Bloomberg has taken that content to the next level by enhancing it with custom authored content from in-house counsel, and integrating it with selected legal content from the Bloomberg Law platform. The one limitation I saw in the platform was that it does not integrate with Microsoft Word, requiring lawyers to cut and paste text. With all the models, precedents, checklists, and templates in the platform, I just hope that Word integration is on the "short list" of upcoming enhancements.

Lex Machina Launches Employment Analytics

JULY 12, 2017

Lex Machina is launching the third new module in the past twelve months, following the release of Securities and Commercial Law products. The new employment litigation module includes over 70,000 discrimination, retaliation, and harassment cases pending in federal court since 2009. According to Lex Machina Chief Evangelist, Owen Byrd, they plan to add Americans with Disabilities Act and labor union cases in the fall.

Employment Law analytics includes the standard Lex Machina data and trend analysis for case timing, resolutions, damages, remedies, and findings, as well as insights into opposing counsel, law firms, parties, judges, and venues which can be used for pitches and litigation strategy.

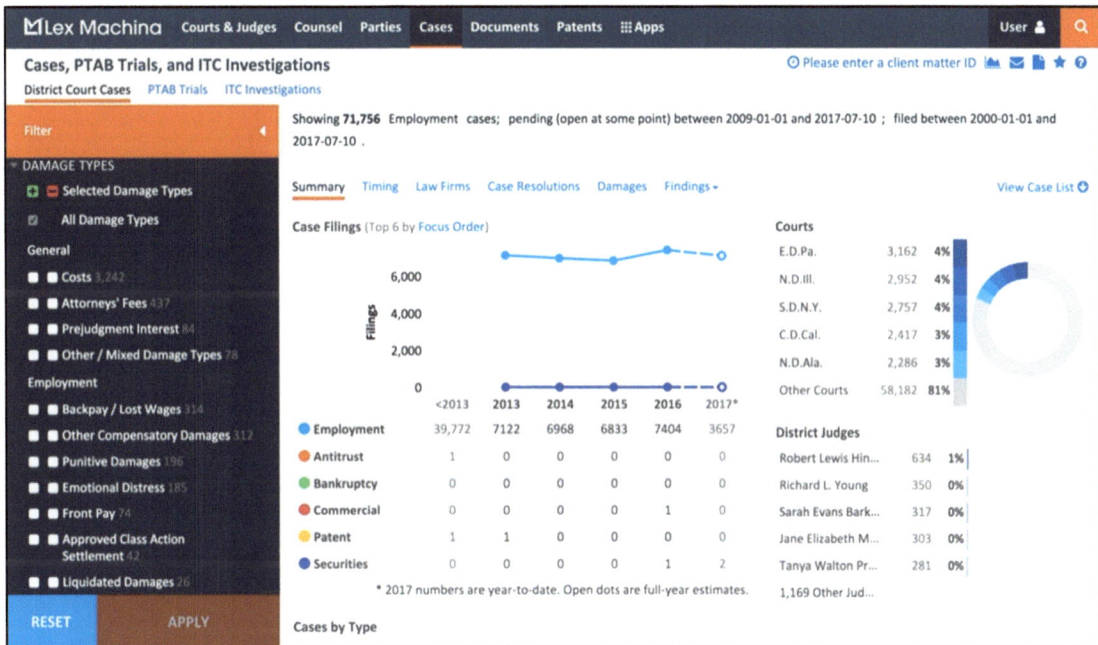

Figure 25: Lex Machina Employment Judgment Events

New content added to Legal Analytics includes three million docket entries and 36 employment-specific tags for damages, findings, and remedies, including:

- **Damages** – Back pay/lost wages, emotional distress, front pay, liquidated damages, and punitive damages.
- **Findings** – Findings under discrimination statues such as Title VII (race/color, religion, national origin, sex/gender), ADEA (age), PDA (pregnancy), §1981/§1983 (equal rights/civil rights violations), USERRA (members of the military), the Equal Pay Act and the Rehabilitation Act. Other findings include: hostile work environment/harassment, retaliation, failure to mitigate defense, time barred defense, failure to accommodate, legitimate nondiscriminatory/non-retaliatory reason defense, and failure to exhaust administrative remedies defense.
- **Remedies** – Notice posting, promotion, and reinstatement. The press release provides some high-level insights derived from Lex Machina's analysis of initial employment litigation findings uncovered by Lex Machina, based on cases filed between January 1, 2009, through June 30, 2017:
  - Discrimination lawsuits are by far the most common (87% of cases), followed by retaliation (66%) and harassment (35%).
  - Employment cases often involve overlapping kinds of claims – discrimination and retaliation claims are combined more than half the time (54%), and the other two combinations occur in about a third of cases.
  - Cases with all three tags comprise just under a quarter of the cases (24%). Top governmental defendants include municipal organizations like the City of New York and the Metropolitan Washington Airport Authority, as well as federal organizations like the U.S. Post Office and Department of Defense.
  - Top corporations by employment cases include companies with a nationwide presence like Wal-Mart, Home Depot, Target, United Parcel Service, Bank of America, and United Airlines.

AALL Exhibit Hall Preview: Themes, Prizes and New Product Showcases from LexisNexis and Bloomberg Law/Bloomberg BNA

JULY 13, 2017

Yesterday I highlighted the AALL Exhibit Hall Offerings of Thomson Reuters and Wolters Kluwer. Today I am highlighting the products, themes, giveaways and games of LexisNexis and Bloomberg Law/Bloomberg BNA which were provided by representatives of each company.

The LexisNexis Products

Here's a sneak peek at what attendees will see at their booth:

- Watch expert analysis with dynamic new video content from litigation guru, James M. Wagstaffe.
- Review smart analytics linked right from a case for revealing insights on judges and litigation parties.
- See how LexisNexis is using artificial intelligence and machine learning technologies to anticipate researcher questions and guide a user to the right information faster.
- Learn how investments in technology and exclusive, essential content are paying big dividends for researchers.

We encourage attendees to check out our must-see **Ravel Law** presentation, the latest addition to our powerful analytics portfolio. We will also preview major enhancements to our **Lexis Practice Advisor** practical guidance solution.

Gifts and Games. Attendees of the AALL Annual Conference will receive a special daily gift for participating in two product demos each day at the booth or by attending a more private Exhibitor Theater Session. Those that view demos will also be entered to win one of three Apple Watch® devices.

Conference participants can earn an extra entry for an Apple Watch by getting a picture taken in our "Advancing Photo Booth." Attendees can have some fun with colleagues, share conference thoughts and post photos on our digital mosaic wall – and watch it come to life. LexisNexis will send participants a complimentary picture as a memento of their time at AALL 2017.

The future of legal research is happening now. And we're saving readers of *Dewey B. Strategic* a front row seat at AALL 2017. LexisNexis hopes to see you in Austin.

Bloomberg Law Bloomberg BNA: "One Platform, One Price, Continuous Innovation."

You have to give them credit, Bloomberg has stuck to its single price for the Bloomberg Law platform, which includes all of Bloomberg BNA, while allowing other customers to opt for Bloomberg BNA practice centers. This year Bloomberg is celebrating: "Our theme is *One Platform. One Price. Continuous Innovation.*"

Product Highlights: The various analytics tools and functionality on the Bloomberg Law platform, their suite of Practical Guidance offerings and their new E-Discovery Practice Center. They will also be previewing an upcoming launch of Legal Principles.

Fun, Games and Giveaways: A photo booth during the opening reception and a t-shirt vending machine will be available in their book. Each day, on the back of six t-shirts in the vending machine they will affix stickers for special prizes including Amazon Echos, American Express gift cards, and Salt Lick BBQ gift cards (Salt Lick is a famous Austin restaurant), among others. One grand prize raffle winner gets $500 to Cavender's, the western wear retail chain headquartered in Tyler, Texas.

The Second Oldest Legal Profession – Law Librarians: The Analytics and Algorithms of Change in the Legal C-Suite

JULY 24, 2017

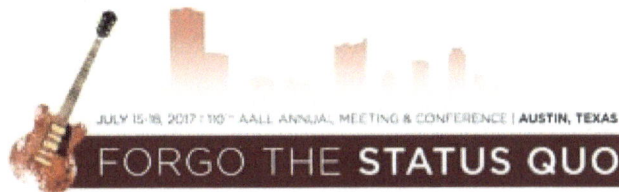

JULY 15-18, 2017 110™ AALL ANNUAL MEETING & CONFERENCE | AUSTIN, TEXAS

FORGO THE **STATUS QUO**

The recent AALL Annual Conference in Austin_was "hands down," the most exciting AALL Program I have ever attended. The programs were great – it was often hard to decide which panel to attend. I found my own panels (Moneyball Analytics and Hits and Misses in New Products) up against programs that I hated to miss (the Innovation Tournament and an "all-star" CEO panel (Fastcase – Walters, Casetext – Heller, Ross – Aruda, Ravel – Lewis) on AI and analytics prodded and provoked by moderator Prof. Susan Nevelow Mart.

Legal Tech thought leaders Bob Ambrogi and Kevin O'Keefe were a familiar sight at the panels, events, exhibits, and the nightly Fastcase after-party). Earlier this week Ambrogi lauded AALL as one of the best conferences for those interested in legal tech. Is the market finally getting what information professionals have known all along? The legal profession requires content experts to navigate the burgeoning market of AI and analytics offerings.

The Second Oldest Legal Profession. I spent time in the exhibit hall with Lexblog's Kevin O'Keefe who commented on the quality and variety of panels and programs at the conference.

O'Keefe was surprised to learn that AALL had been around since 1906. In fact, in the legal community, only the American Bar Association has an earlier founding... 1878. AALL predates every other law-related association by decades. It was 65 years before the Association of Legal Administrators was founded in 1971, 74 years before ILTA in 1980, and 79 years before the Legal Marketing Association was founded in 1985.

O'Keefe also commented on the importance of information professionals by comparison to other law firm administrative functions. "Lawyers could still practice law without technology, or marketing, or administrative help, but legal information always was and remains core to the practice of law."

O'Keefe has a point which goes beyond the core practice of law. Law firms have become complex, regional, national, and multi-national organizations. Business intelligence and legal knowledge has never been more critical to the current high stakes competitive market. No one else in the firm is better qualified to assess the potential value of research products offering AI and analytics... and yet... information professionals occupy relatively few seats in the legal C-Suite compared to the technologists and marketing professionals. The person who understands the quality of information should be at the table and not down the organizational chart out of earshot.

But this may be about to change...

The Hidden Algorithms and Analytics of Change: The Rise of the CKO

I have been a law librarian long enough to remember that back in the 1980s there was an explosion of demand for information professionals in law firms. Online research was emerging as a core practice need and national law firms saw the benefit of creating national director positions to develop information strategies and manage the eye bulging cost of national online research contracts. Law firms began to compete for talent! Law librarians spent a decade as peers to their relatively junior or at least newly minted colleagues in IT. By the mid-1990s firms began to create C-level positions, often Information Technology Directors invited into the C-Suite, while Directors of Information Resources/Libraries were left behind and routinely slotted into a variety of subordinate reporting relationships from operations to finance to technology. Now that there are powerful emerging technologies such as analytics and AI that require content expertise, law librarians and knowledge mangers are positioned for a professional renaissance.

In July, *The American Lawyer* published their rebranded annual survey of law libraries. "In our newly renamed Survey of Law Firm Knowledge Management, Library, and Research Professionals, we found these information professionals are increasingly focused on data and analytical tools to provide cutting-edge research for their firm." The survey was published along with two articles entitled "Law Librarian Try Chief Knowledge Officer" (http://www.americanlawyer.com/id=1202791116149/Law-Librarian-Try-Chief-Knowledge-Officer) and "From

Providing Data to Providing Insight" (http://www.americanlawyer.com/id=1202791117753/From-Providing-Data-to-Providing-Insight).

In addition, Greg Lambert, the Chief Knowledge Officer at Jackson Walker in Houston, is the first CKO to be elected President of AALL. Greg is a well-known blogger and co-creator of the Three Geeks and a Law Blog. He will no doubt be a strong voice for the profession and a living reminder that a new breed of information professionals is in town. In his first address to the Association, Lambert noted as he has before: "Law librarians and others in the legal information profession are some of the smartest and most credentialed members of their organizations. However, this does very little when you're not part of the decision-making team. A local Houston politician once told me, 'If you are not at the table, you are on the menu.' She is right. It is time to go beyond being smart and credentialed, and helpful and nice. It is time we take action and create success for ourselves, our profession, our Association, our work place, and the entire legal profession."

Can Law Librarians Save Legal Education? Law school enrollments have been trending down. The problem is not just the tight job market for traditional legal jobs. The bigger problem may be the reluctance of law schools to transform the curriculum – tenured professors cannot be forced to integrate the latest technology of legal practice into their syllabi. Students are being asked to pay top dollar and carry a spectacular long-term loan burden for an education which is still rooted in the 19th century. Several of last week's AALL Conference programs highlighted the numerous ways in which academic law library directors are transforming their law libraries into tech laboratories in order to give students access to the technologies they need for today's legal practice... which are not embraced by the rest of the faculty.

Stay tuned. "The times they are a changing..." and if you want to keep up... show up for the 2018 Annual AALL Meeting in Baltimore, Maryland, with the theme "From Knowledge to Action." It will be the 111th AALL Annual Conference... how's that for depth of expertise and endurance!

Breaking News on Bad Data: Thomson Reuters Discovers Data Error in Their Monitor Suite Litigation Analytics

AUGUST 1, 2017

This morning I talked with Andrew Martens, Global Head of Product and U.S. Editorial at Thomson Reuters, who advised me that the company had discovered and corrected a data error in their Litigation analytics in the Monitor Suite platform which impacted data between mid-April and July 2017.

What products were affected? Litigation Monitor data in the Monitor Suite platform.

What content was affected? Federal district court data only.

Other federal and state court data was not impacted? According to Martens the impacted data represents less than 1.4 percent of their district court docket archive.

What products were not impacted? Thomson Reuters also provides docket data on the Westlaw platform through Courtwire. This is a separate docket data stream and it was not impacted. "State dockets, all state and federal opinions, as well as all intellectual property and deals content were not impacted. Dockets on Westlaw were not affected and were current at all times."

Help Is Available. In addition to offering an apology, Thomson Reuters is offering some support.

"We are happy to help rerun or supplement your Monitor Suite reports. Please contact your Business Development Consultant at (877) 347-6360 or our Reference Attorneys at (800) 733-2889 if you would like assistance."

The problem of Multiple Data Streams. Thomson Reuters is not alone getting burned by the management of multiple data streams. Earlier this year LexisNexis was sued when a customer found errors in a paperback code volume. I also asked at that time why LexisNexis would not have a single stream of statutory and regulatory changes feeding into all of their products.

Is there any risk for law firms? Generally this type of litigation analytics is used for pitches and not for client support activities. It is not impossible that the data could have been used in some client support context, e.g. litigation strategy. In this case, TR benefits from not having rolled their analytics into their main Westlaw product as competitors Bloomberg Law and LexisNexis have. Since the Monitor Suite is normally used by research and competitive intelligence specialists, it will be easier to review any use of the data during the April to July period to determine if reports need to be rerun. Firms which have a resources monitoring system such as Research Monitor or Onelog will find it very easy to identify users and usage during the impacted period.

Here is the letter that TR is sending to their customers:

Dear Jean,

We are writing to make you aware of a recent issue relating to the currentness of one of our data sets in our business development tool – Litigation Monitor, part of Monitor Suite. We recognize that having current information is important to our customers, and we apologize for this issue.

A gap in the federal district court docket collection of Litigation Monitor was found, and the issue has been addressed, bringing the collection back to our normal currency expectations. State dockets, all state and federal opinions, as well as all intellectual property and deals content were not impacted. Dockets on Westlaw were not affected and were current at all times.

The Litigation Monitor issue began as a result of an enhancement project across our dockets collection. These enhancements were immediately available on Westlaw but required additional processing for Monitor Suite. This additional processing resulted in a backlog in loading federal district court dockets to Litigation Monitor.

If you ran Litigation Monitor reports using federal court docket data since mid-April, please know that your data set may have been incomplete and the report may have been impacted. Accessing Litigation Monitor's quicklinks and enhanced portal links will return current data. We are happy to help rerun or supplement your Monitor Suite reports. Please contact your Business Development Consultant at (877) 347-6360 or our Reference Attorneys at (800) 733-2889 if you would like assistance.

We sincerely apologize for the data delay and for not informing you sooner. The team misjudged the time to resolution, and as a result did not keep you adequately informed of this coverage issue. We have resolved the data issue and reinforced our internal escalation process, and you can be confident that Litigation Monitor is current.

Sincerely,

Andy Martens

Wolters Kluwer Partners with KM Standards and Launches AI Workflow Tool: M&A Clause Analytics

August 1, 2017

Wolters Kluwer Legal & Regulatory U.S. continues to release new products and features with astonishing regularity.

On July 24th, they released ***M&A Clause Analytics***, a new workflow tool which combines machine learning and human expert curation to streamline the M&A drafting process. The product is designed to help lawyers quickly locate the best model documents and clauses. Wolters Kluwer Partnered with Kingsley Martin of KM Standards to develop a statistical analysis of 17000 documents from WK's RB Source database of SEC Filings. According to the press release the product is designed in response to a legal market focused on enhancing "quality, efficiency, and ease of preparing merger and acquisition agreements." M&A Analytics which covers 13 document types, will be a central component of the *Transactional Law Suite for Securities*.

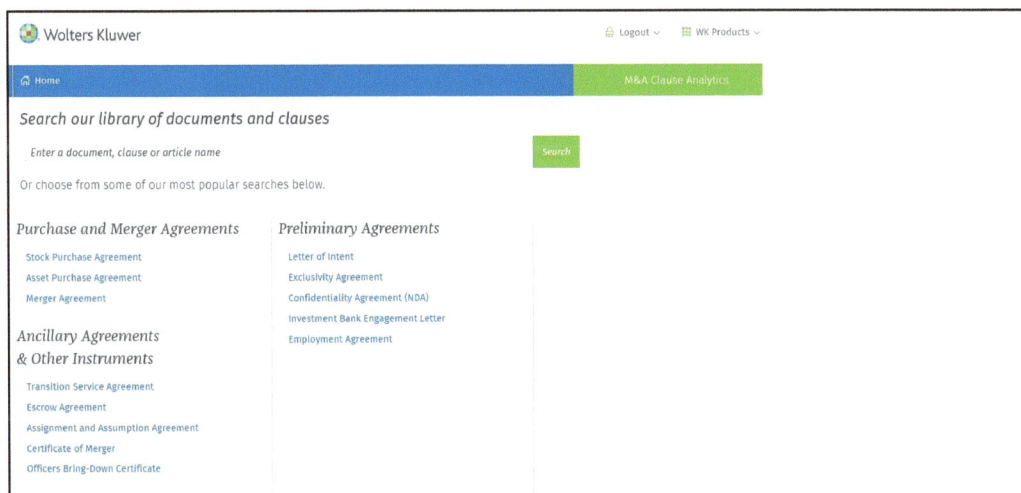

Figure 26: M&A Clause Analytics Home Page

"Model forms reliably capture best practice standards, which can be used as a starting point for drafting a new agreement or selected clauses," said Kingsley

Martin, President and CEO of KMStandards. "Using our proprietary technology, the forms and clauses are assembled from the automated analysis of thousands of successfully negotiated agreements which importantly provides an objective, statistical standard that gives lawyers with an immediate sense of which clauses tend to be highly negotiated and which are not, providing important context that aids them in drafting." Martin is a seasoned KM pioneer whose experience includes KM development in several ALM 100 firms and KM product development for legal giant Thomson Reuters and is well known to many information professionals.

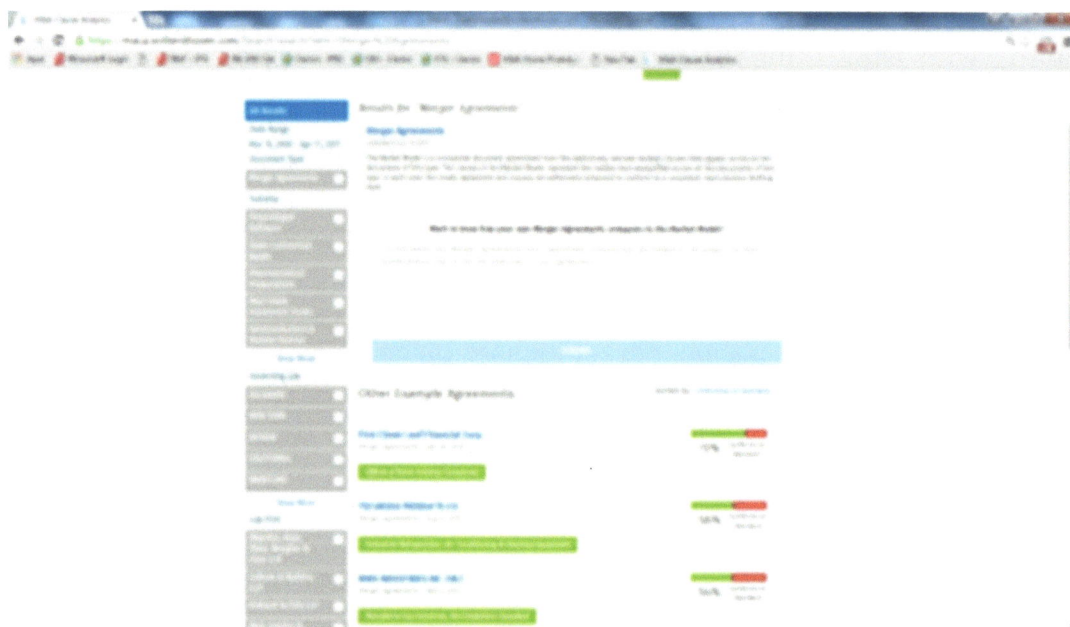

Figure 27: Clause Analytics Compared to Market

A Different Kind of Analytics. Researchers are becoming familiar with a variety of new analytics tools in the form of rings, bars, lines, and maps. The KM Standards visualization provides a color-coded score based on how closely the designated text or document matches the market standard. Analytics is at work behind the scenes scoring the documents and clauses for conformity to market standards.

M&A Clause Analytics leverages the database of SEC documents from the WK RB Source Filings product which includes thousands of Merger, Stock Purchase, and Asset Purchase Agreements and their ancillary documents. *M&A Clause Analytics provides* a model for each agreement type based on a statistically significant sample set of recent documents. "The AI-generated statistical median model document is then carefully reviewed by M&A attorneys, ensuring the best of machine learning and expert human curation."

Core functionalities include:

- Comparing documents or clauses with what's "market standard."
- Conforming clauses to market standard.
- Providing contextual practice guidance.

M&A Clause Analytics' most notable features include the following:

- **Search** Users can locate "on-point" agreements and clauses from the exhibit archive by searching or browsing amongst the 13 types of documents in the database and seamlessly benchmarking documents or clauses.
- **Filters** enable users to focus of specific tags and clause types.
- **Benchmarking** Color coded graphical symbols signal the extent to which the structure of each document or clause conforms to the market.
- **Select and analyze** An agreement functionality enables users to quickly determine how closely a selected agreement's clauses conform to the market standard.

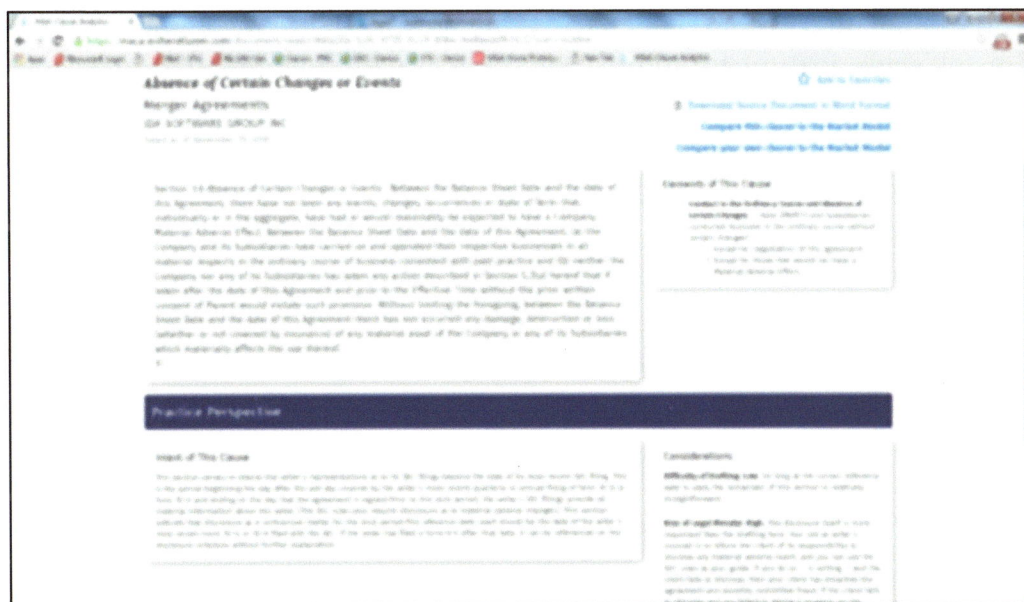

Figure 28: Practice Perspectives

- **Practice perspectives** offers practical guidance written by M&A attorneys. for each clause providing and analysis of 3 key issues: difficulty of drafting, legal mistake/risk, and standard versus negotiated. Where any of these considerations are beyond the norm, they are clearly identified.

- **Analyze Your Own Document or Clause**. A document or clause can be cut and pasted into dashboard and the analytics engine will perform a clausal comparison of the entire document or clause to the market standard.

Dean Sonderegger summed up the value of M&A Clause Analytics in the press release: "As clients continue to aggressively pursue improved cost efficiency and timeliness from legal providers, legal professionals are increasingly in need of workflow solutions that address their most critical pain points. We developed M&A Clause Analytics to harness the newest enabling technology in combination with our domain expertise to provide legal professionals with greater clarity, efficiency, and understanding of Merger Agreements that they confront most frequently in practice."

Suggestions – The M&A Clause Analytics has similar functionality to the Bloomberg Law Corporate Transactions product which I reviewed in 2015. The Bloomberg product leverages a larger set of SEC documents, but lacks the human vetting offered by the Wolters Kluwer product. The Bloomberg Law product also offers filtering on more criteria, but executives from Wolters Kluwer assured me that additional filters will be added in the near future. I also recommend that they add a foldering feature to allow a lawyer to save their analyzed clauses and documents. The release of the M&A Clause Analyzer following the recent launch of SmartTasks demonstrates that Wolters Kluwer is focused on building a variety of workflow tools which complement their established strength in supporting regulatory legal practices.

Bloomberg Law Launches 15th Practice Center: E-Discovery

AUGUST 9, 2017

Today Bloomberg Law is announcing the release of its 15th practice center which is focused on E-Discovery. Bloomberg is moving rapidly to consolidate existing BNA news, practice and analytical resources, as well as creating new content to enhance attorneys' workflow efficiency. The Bloomberg Law Practice Centers are designed to compete directly with incumbents in this space: Thomson Reuters Practical Law and Lexis Practice Advisor.

Figure 29: Bloomberg Law E-Discovery Practice Center

The E-Discovery Practice Center offers a comprehensive solution that integrates news, primary sources including both published and unpublished state and federal court opinions, tools, sample forms, and expert guidance. The press release indicates that this is the only resource of its kind available on an integrated legal research and business intelligence platform. The E-Discovery Practice Center will be available to all Bloomberg Law subscribers at no additional cost.

The Practice Center's home page features high value content including a curated collection of fully searchable state and federal court opinions, state-specific discovery guidance and rules, and BNA's E-Discovery Portfolio series. I don't recall seeing a collection of state e-discovery rules in any other product. Since e-discovery touches on a wide range of complex issues, the E-Discovery Center links to other Bloomberg BNA materials in related disciplines, including: cross-border data transfers, government and internal investigations, and data and privacy security.

The E-Discovery Stages page walks practitioners through the various stages and issues they will face during E-Discovery. Stages include: Preservation, Production, Privilege, and Costs.

E-DISCOVERY

E-Discovery Stages ☆ Favorite

General E-Discovery Practice

eData Deskbook (Morgan Lewis)
Electronic Discovery Practice Under the Federal Rules
Guerrilla Discovery (James)
Handling Federal Discovery (James)
Managing Discovery of Electronic Information (FJC)
Manual for Complex Litigation (FJC)
E-Discovery Practice Tools

Preservation

LEGAL ANALYSIS

Preserving Electronically Stored Information: A Practical Approach
Records Retention for Enterprise Knowledge Management
Spoliation in the Electronic Age

PRACTICE TOOLS: SAMPLE HOLD NOTICES TO CLIENT

Litigation Hold Notice and FAQs
Legal Hold Notice
Litigation Hold Notice
Preservation Notice
Preservation Letter to Client
Litigation Hold Reminder Notice
Certification Regarding Litigation Hold Compliance
Form Q&A to Provide to Hold-Notice Recipients
Litigation Hold Re: Social Media

PRACTICE TOOLS: SAMPLE HOLD NOTICES TO OTHER PARTIES

Preservation Letter to Opposing Counsel or Non-Represented Party
Preservation Letter to Opposing Counsel
Letter to Opposing Counsel Demanding Preservation
Preservation Letter to Third Party Contractor
Spoliation/Preservation Interrogatories

PRACTICE TOOLS: LITIGATION HOLD PROCEDURES

Critical Steps Checklist Upon Reasonable Anticipation of Litigation
Sample IT Legal Hold Procedures
Sample Data Hold Log
Sample Preservation Order

PRACTICE TOOLS: RECORD RETENTION

Sample Document Retention Policy
Creating a Records Retention Plan
Sample Records Retention Plan
Records Retention Employee Acknowledgement
Sample Social Media Clause in Document Retention Policy
Retention Period for Specific Records
Laws & Regulations re: Records Retention

Search & Retrieval

LEGAL ANALYSIS

Data Management (Wiley)
Evidence Gathering in the Age of ESI (White Collar)
Internal Corporate Investigations: Gathering Documents (ABA)

PRACTICE TOOLS

Sample Custodian Questionnaire and Checklist for Collecting ESI
Sample Upjohn Warning
Vendor Checklist
Adaptable for E-Discovery Practice

Subject Matter-Specific E-Discovery Materials

Bloomberg Law Bankruptcy Treatise
Employment Discrimination Law (Bloomberg BNA)
Employment Evidence (James)
Fraud and Forensics (ABI)
Patent Litigation Strategies (Bloomberg BNA)
Trademark Litigation (Bloomberg BNA)

Production

LEGAL ANALYSIS

Insiders' Guide to Technology - Assisted Review (Wiley)
Technology-Assisted Review for Discovery Requests (FJC)

PRACTICE TOOLS

Sample Questions for Clients Regarding Historic Document Collection
Checklist for Rule 26 Meeting Preparation
Sample Motion to Compel
Sample Expert Declaration re: Inaccessibility/Burden
Sample Document Request
Request for Production of Documents
Sample Quick Peek Agreement
Stipulated Protective Order
Sample Clawback Agreement
Sample Demand for Return of Inadvertently Produced Privileged Materials

Privilege

E-Discovery Cases: Privilege

LAWS & RULES

Fed. R. Evid. 502

LEGAL ANALYSIS

ABA/BNA Lawyers' Manual on Professional Conduct

BLOOMBERG BNA PORTFOLIOS

Attorney-Client Privilege and Work-Product Doctrine: Corporate Applications
In-House Corporate Counsel and the Attorney-Client Privilege
Privilege Issues in the Age of Electronic Discovery

PRACTICE TOOLS

Sample Privilege Log
Privilege Log

Costs & Sanctions

LEGAL ANALYSIS

Spoliation in the Electronic Age
The Law and Tactics of Sanctions

PRACTICE TOOLS

Sample Motion for Spoliation Sanctions
Sample Motion for Spoliation Sanctions
Sample Declaration in Opposition to Spoliation Sanctions
Sample Declaration of Good Faith in Response to Sanctions Motion
Spoliation Sanctions by Circuit

State-Specific E-Discovery Materials

California (James)
Connecticut (MCLE)
Illinois Pretrial Practice (James)
Massachusetts Discovery Practice (MCLE)
Massachusetts E-Discovery and Evidence: Preservation Through Trial (MCLE)
Massachusetts Expert Witnesses: Digital Discovery (MCLE)
Massachusetts Superior Court Civil Practice Manual (MCLE)
New Hampshire (MCLE)
New Jersey (NJICLE)
New York (James)
Oregon (Oregon State Bar)
Rhode Island (MCLE)
Texas (James)
Texas - Deceptive Trade Practices Act (James)
Texas - Employment Law (James)

Figure 30: The E-Discovery Stages page

Wolters Kluwer Preparing to Help Lawyers Predict Legislative Changes with New AI Features

SEPTEMBER 7, 2017

Wolters Kluwer

I was beginning to wonder if Wolters Kluwer Law & Regulatory was planning to take a rest from their aggressive schedule of innovation. Well I was wrong, I just learned that WK is preparing to introduce predictive analytics for federal legislation in their Federal Knowledge Center. The legislative analytics will be powered by artificial intelligence tools developed in collaboration with Skopos Labs, Inc., a software company specializing in predictive analytics.

Since the beginning of 2017 Wolters Kluwer has announced a dizzying variety of enhancements, alliances, and products including SmartTasks for corporate know how, The Federal Legislative Knowledge Center – a new cybersecurity product, and alliance with ktMINE to offer IP analytics, and a partnership with KMStandards to launch an AI workflow tool for M&A clause analytics.

The Federal Developments Knowledge Center was designed by Wolters Kluwer to serve as a comprehensive tool to provide lawyers with deeper insights into proposed legislation and regulation. Features include: SmartCharts, breaking news, primary source documents, and impact analysis on executive orders, regulations, and legislation.

Since statutes and regulations have always been the backbone of Wolters Kluwer's suite of products, the application of predictive analytics to this core strength is a logical product trajectory.

S.1002 Community Lending Enhancement and Regulatory Relief Act of 2017

OFFICIAL CONGRESSIONAL SUMMARY

Would give top U.S. agricultural and food officials permanent representation on the Committee on Foreign Investment in the United States (CFIUS) and include new agriculture and food related criteria for the CFIUS to consider when reviewing transactions that could result in control of a U.S. business by a foreign company.

WOLTERS KLUWER COMMENTARY

EFFECTIVE DATE/STATUS:

On May 2, 2017, the bill was referred to the House Committee on Energy and Commerce.

SYNOPSIS:

Would give top U.S. agricultural and food officials permanent representation on the Committee on Foreign Investment in the United States (CFIUS) and include new agriculture and food related criteria for the CFIUS to consider when reviewing transactions that could result in control of a U.S. business by a foreign company.

IMPACT/NEXT STEP:

Top federal agricultural and food officials would be permanently added CFIUS, which currently does not include permanent representation from the U.S. Department of Agriculture or the U.S. Department of Health and Human Services.

STATEMENT OF ADMINISTRATION:

The Administration strongly supports House passage of S.J.Res. 34, which would nullify the Federal Communications Commission's final rule titled "Protecting the Privacy of Customers of Broadband and Other Telecommunication Services." 81 Fed. Reg. 87274 (December 2, 2016).

VIEW ORIGINAL DOCUMENT

S. 1002 Community Lending Enhancement and Regulatory Relief Act of 2017. May 2, 2017

BILL BREAKDOWN Powered by Skopos Labs

Became Law

TEXT ANALYSIS

(House Rules)(Rep. Frelinghuysen, R-NJ) This Statement of Administration Policy provides views on the House amendment to amendments to H.R. 244, which contains the text of the Consolidated Appropriations Act, 2017. The Administration appreciates the bill's provision of

READ FULL TEXT ANALYSIS

EXTERNAL FACTORS

PREDICTIVE OUTLOOK

Likelihood of passing chamber — 1%

Likelihood of becoming law — 1%

ADDITIONAL BILL DETAILS

SIMILAR BILLS INTRODUCED IN THIS CONGRESS	SIMILAR BILLS INTRODUCED IN PREVIOUS CONGRESSIONAL SESSIONS	U.S.C. CITATIONS WITHIN THIS BILL
H.R.676 - Expanded & Improved Medicare For All Act	H.R.1003	38 U.S.C. Chapter 11
H.R.2313 - Small Business Relief and Job Creation Act	H.R.2104	42 U.S.C. 401et seq.
H.R.370 - To repeal the Patient Protection and Affordable Care Act	H.R.574	38 U.S.C. 1114

Predictive AI for Legislation. The AI enhancements will enable lawyers to quickly assess proposed legislation, and predict its likelihood of passage in the chamber of the Congress in which it presently resides, as well as its likelihood of ultimate enactment (passage by both chambers and the signature of the President).

The analytics, which will be available this fall within Federal Developments Knowledge Center have been developed using natural language processing of the legal text and computational assessment of hundreds of external positive and negative factors that affect a particular bill. The tool also provides background on a bill's relationship to similar legislation and relevant sections of The Code of Laws of the United States.

Analytics as Differentiator. Analytics offerings are becoming a "must have" enhancement for legal research products. "Analytics competency" is also becoming a differentiator for lawyers and law firm in the business and practice of law. I look forward to learning more about this innovative new predictive analytics product from Wolters Kluwer and Skopos Labs.

LexisNexis Announces Lexis Practice Advisor Transactional Search Powered by Intelligize and Other LPA Enhancements

SEPTEMBER 19, 2017

LexisNexis has spent the past five years on a treasure hunt, acquiring some of the most innovative legal tech startups. My refrain in every post about these acquisitions has been: "When and how will LexisNexis start integrating the key features of these products into their existing product lines?" Today LexisNexis is announcing important enhancements to Lexis Practice Advisor, leveraging their acquisition of Intelligize in September 2016. Additional enhancements to Lexis Practice Advisor include a new and more intuitive home page, enhanced navigation, and post navigation filtering. The new Home page enables lawyers to begin their navigation by jurisdiction or topic.

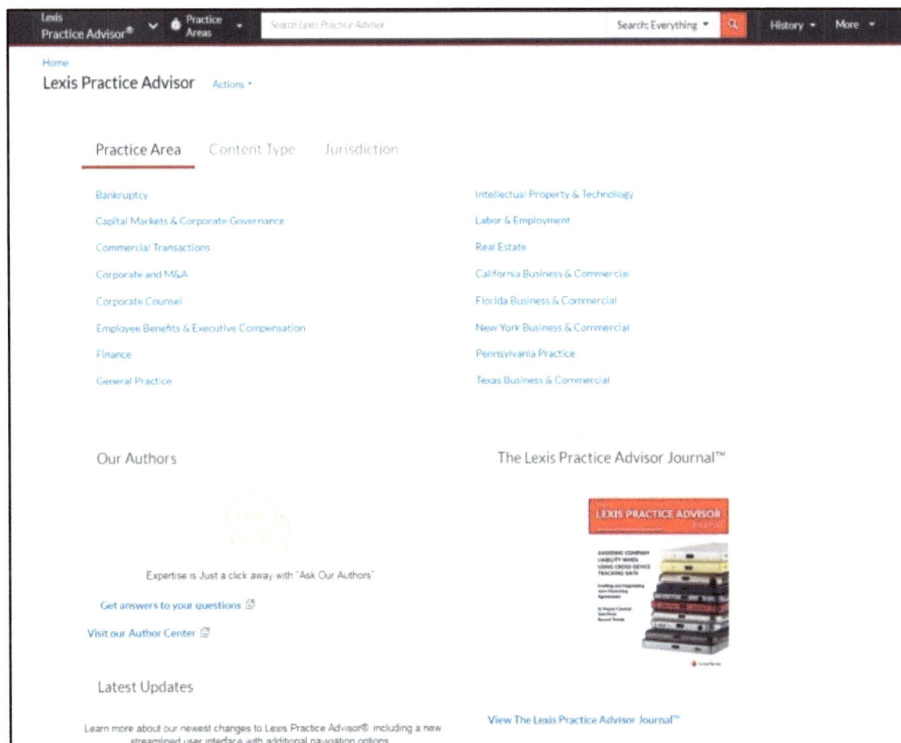

Figure 31: New Lexis Practice Advisor Home Page

The new interface enables users to navigate content by practice area, content type, or jurisdiction. In addition, content is organized along a task-based hierarchical tree, which allows users to either browse a comprehensive collection of practice area content or quickly drill down to find more nuanced, specific results.

LPA currently includes guidance such as practice notes, annotated forms, clauses, and checklists across multiple practice areas, including: Capital Markets & Corporate Governance, Commercial Transactions, Corporate and M&A, Intellectual Property & Technology, Labor & Employment, Real Estate, and Finance. The editorial team is developing eight new practice modules. The LPA content is created by more than 650 expert practitioners from over 265 law firms and organizations.

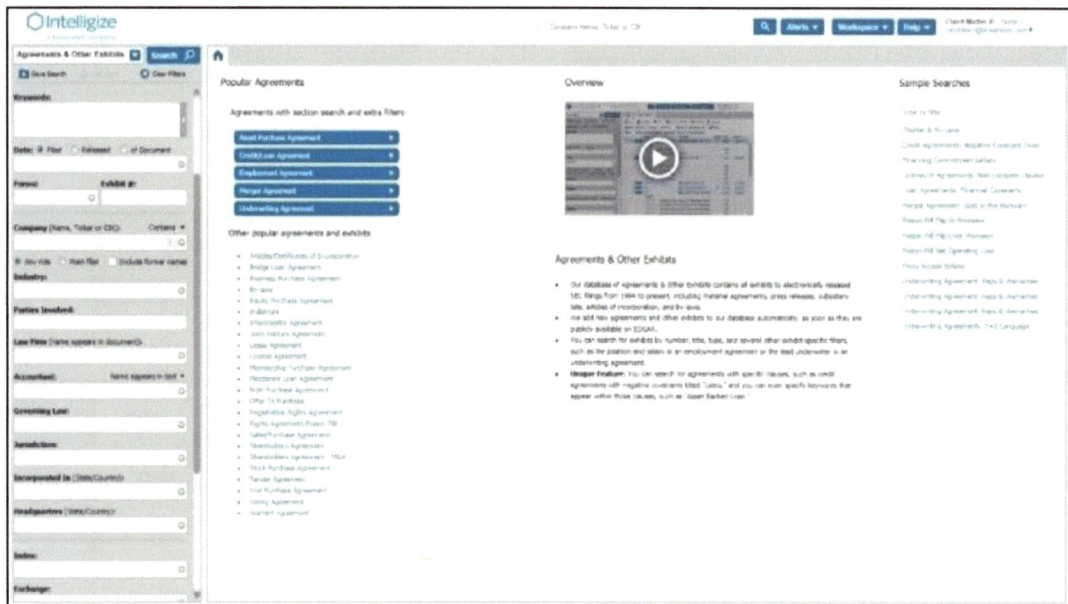

Figure 32: Transactional Search Powered by Intelligize

Transactional Search Powered by Intelligize

Intelligize includes over 15,000 M&A transactions, 15,000 registered offerings, 8,000 exempt filings, and international prospectuses not found in EDGAR, and all EDGAR-filed exhibits since 1994. Transactional Search Powered by Intelligize will deliver results based on Intelligize analytics which integrates "how-to guidance" with "market samples," filings, and clauses. Search and navigation tools include embedded videos and a list of "common searches" enabling lawyers to leverage other peoples "know how."

How Current? One of the most important editorial features in any product is the notation regarding its updates. LPA includes a "reviewed on" date which signals the currency of the content.

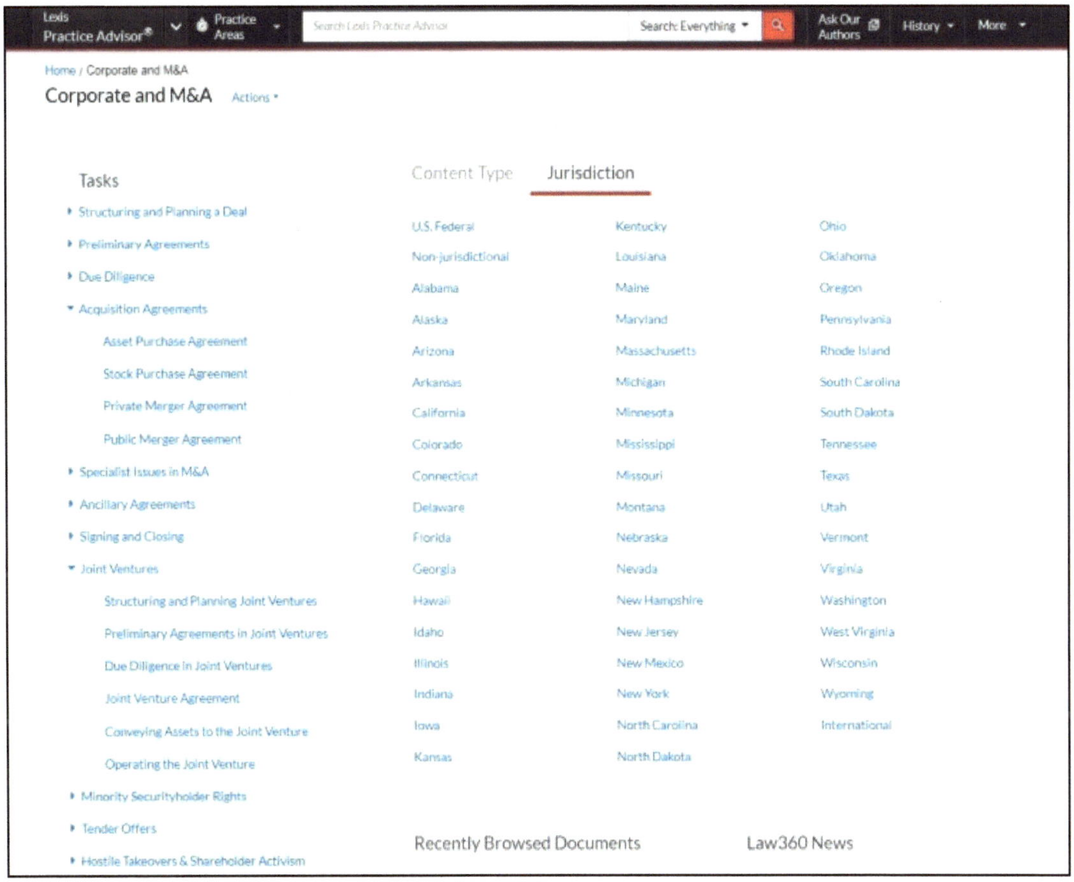

Figure 33: LPA M&A Workflow Tasks and Jurisdictions.

What Do I Think They Should Do Next?

1. Integrate with Microsoft Word so lawyers can more easily draft and edit while using LPA.
2. Integrate with Lex Machina and Ravel Law (other recent LexisNexis acquisitions). Wouldn't it be interesting to also know which types of contracts have been the subject of litigation and the "moneyball" outcomes related to specific documents and clauses in specific jurisdictions?

3. Try to identify the law firm which drafted the SEC exhibits. While SEC filings can be located by law firm, the exhibits are a goldmine of additional know-how and model documents for a vast spectrum of documents such as commercial leases and executive compensation documents. Law firms still struggle with internal knowledge management and offering the ability to filter a larger set of documents by law firm would be a welcome enhancement.

Lex Machina Launches Bankruptcy Appeals Analytics Module

SEPTEMBER 26, 2017

Today Lex Machina is releasing a new module which covers district court bankruptcy appeals. Until now all prior Lex Machina modules have focused on federal trials. The Bankruptcy product covers 18,000 bankruptcy appeals filed since 2009. This is Lex Machina's first foray into appellate analytics.

The Lex Machina CTO, Karl Harris, is quoted in the press release: "Although there are relatively few bankruptcy appeals cases at the district court level compared to commercial or employment litigation cases, the stakes are incredibly high for all those involved, so it is imperative that attorneys know the lay of the land before entering the courtroom. With Lex Machina, attorneys will now be able to get critical insights into the behaviors of district court judges, allowing them to provide the most informed counsel and formulate the best case strategy."

Bankruptcy practice is highly specialized and Lex Machina developed the new module based on feedback received from top bankruptcy litigators. The new product incorporates 10 practice-specific tags and 15 unique "dispute appeals" categories, which will enable attorneys derive insights a competitive advantage throughout the appeals process. Since bankruptcy appeals are much less common than traditional appeals it is more challenging for attorneys to gain insights into judges and outcomes.

As part of the product development process, Lex Machina interviewed top bankruptcy appeals lawyers to better understand their needs and incorporated their feedback directly into the new offering. As a result Lex Machina developed 10 new filers and 15 appellate categories.

- The new case tags include: Bankruptcy Appeal, Individual Debtor, Business Debtor, Adversary Proceeding, Chapter 7, Chapter 9, Chapter 11, Chapter 12, Chapter 13, and Chapter 15.
- The new dispute appeals categories include: Procedure and Jurisdiction, Malfeasance and Remedies, Officers, Administration, Lift of Automatic Stay, Debtor's Rights and Duties, Plan and Disclosure Statements, Objection to Confirmation, Property of the Estate, Dismissal and

Conversion, Discharge and Dischargeability, Claims and Liens, Objection to Proof of Claim, Avoidance, and State or Other Federal Law.

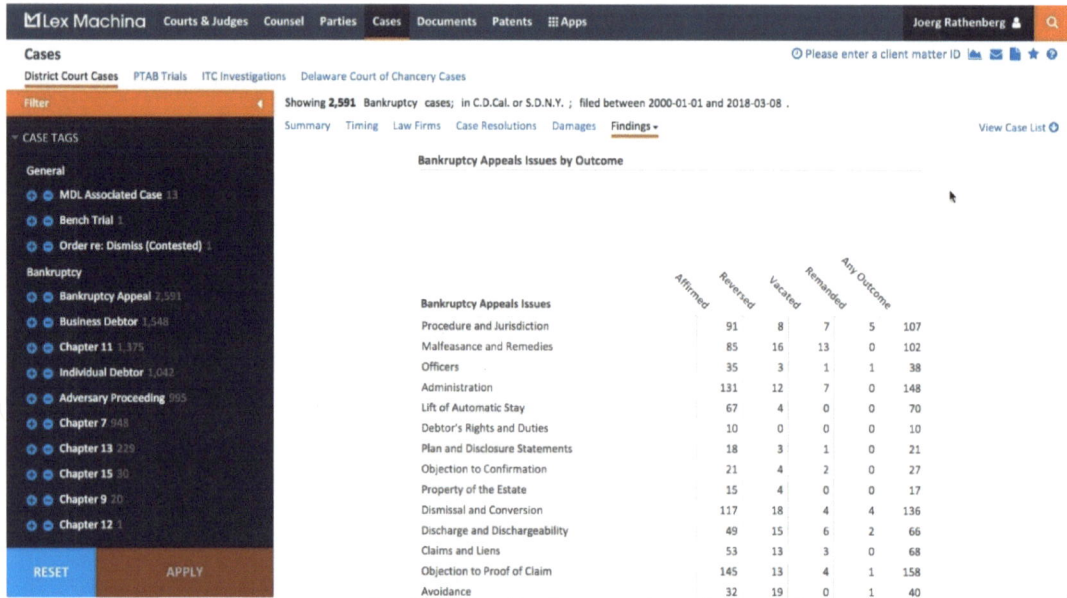

Figure 34: Lex Machina Bankruptcy Appeals Analytics

Unique Insights

Owen Byrd, the chief evangelist and general counsel at Lex Machina, provided me with a preview of the product. One of my favorite things about seeing a new Lex Machina module is hearing Byrd exclaim, "No one has ever seen this data before!" Byrd highlights some of the unique insights of the bankruptcy product in the press release: "If you're a creditor trying to decide whether or not to file an appeal, knowing whether a particular judge has a tendency to affirm or reverse the lower court's ruling will have a significant impact on your appeal strategy. Similarly, having concrete data at your fingertips about the expertise of opposing counsel or how often larger creditors, such as banks, win their appeals could weigh heavily into your decision-making."

Bankruptcy Appeals Report

Lex Machina will be releasing a comprehensive report on district court bankruptcy appeals in October, containing insights and analyses of bankruptcy appeals cases filed between January 1, 2009, and September 30, 2017. The company also released a blog post today (https://lexmachina.com/lex-machina-launches-legal-analytics-for-bankruptcy-appeals-in-district-court/) that provides a sample of data points to be featured in the upcoming report, including:

- More than 17,000 cases have been pending since 2009.
- Nationally, U.S. District Court judges are more likely to affirm the Bankruptcy Court's decision (30% of cases pending since 2009) than to reverse, remand, and/or vacate (7%).
- The most common issues in bankruptcy appeals include Administration, Objection to Proof of Claim, and Dismissal and Conversion.

Bloomberg Law Launches AI-Enabled Research Features: Points of Law and Citation Maps

OCTOBER 3, 2017

In late September Bloomberg Law announced several new research features which leverage artificial intelligence and machine learning technologies to accelerate case law research. The new "Points of Law" feature allows attorneys to quickly find language critical to a court's reasoning to support their legal arguments. This feature was immediately available to all current subscribers to Bloomberg Law at no additional cost.

The Bloomberg Law platform now features one million points of law and is updated throughout the day. "Points of Law" results are generated by the application of machine learning to the Bloomberg Law database of 13 million published and unpublished state and federal court opinions. Researchers can either start their research with a point of law or start with a keyword then sort by relevance or most cited.

This new feature was created in response to market demand for workflow enhancing tools. "Points of Law" research results highlight the relevant language in each opinion. The press release describes the benefit as "enabling attorneys to shorten their research time and quickly identify the best language to strengthen legal arguments."

Points of Law. From a case, users can navigate seamlessly among points of law and can also augment their research with related points of law and with relevant citing cases shown as a list or an interactive timeline via the Citation Map feature.

The Citation Map provides a visualization of most cited cases, relationships among key cases, and changes over time for the point of law at issue. This is a radical departure from traditional notions of a citator.

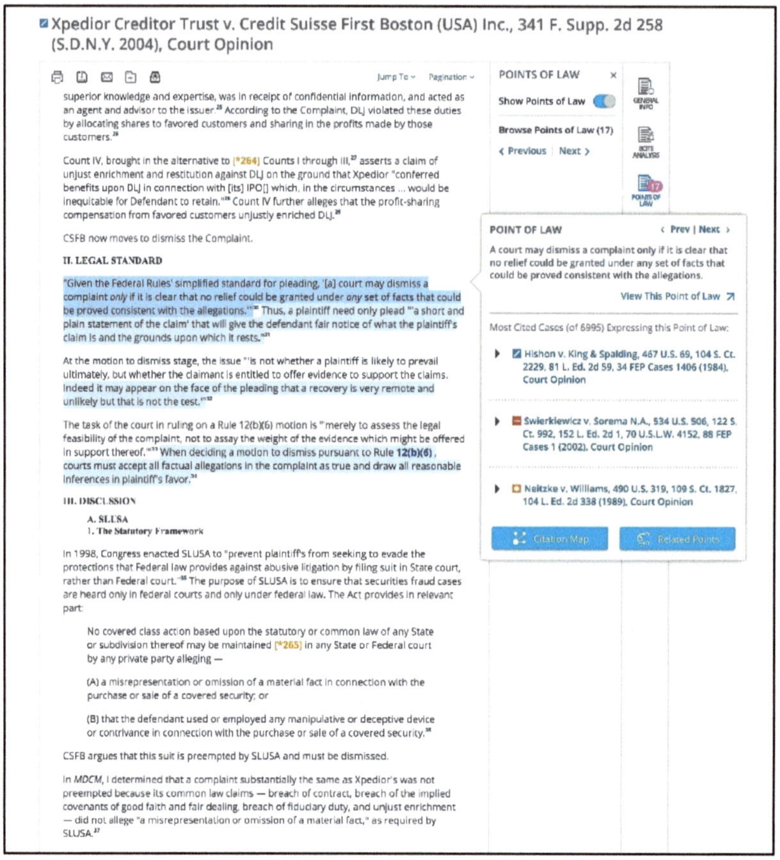

Figure 35: Bloomberg Law Points of Law

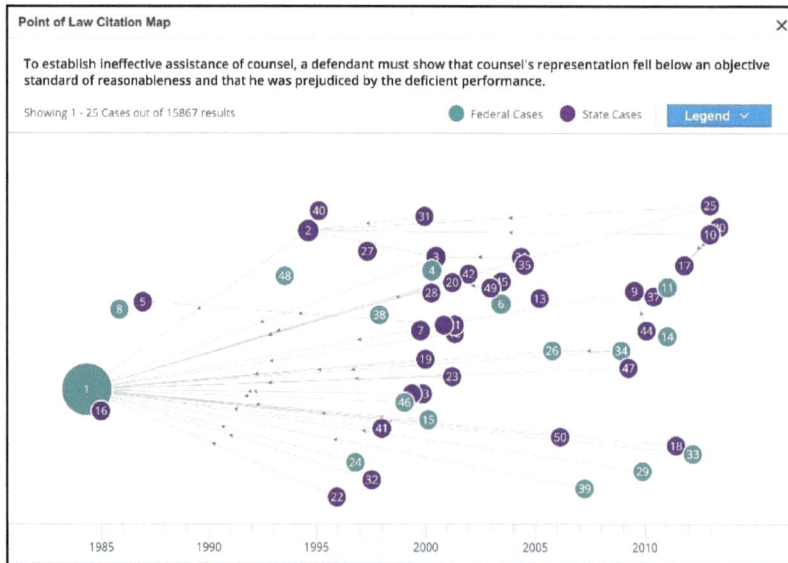

Figure 36: The Bloomberg Law Citation Map

Search and Filter. The system also supports familiar search techniques for narrowing focus including keyword search and jurisdictional filters.

"Points of Law is another example of our commitment to continuous innovation and ongoing investment in data and technology to empower attorneys to more effectively and efficiently advise their clients," said Scott Mozarsky, President of Bloomberg Law. "With Points of Law, we have streamlined and improved the legal research process using machine learning and data visualization to reveal previously undiscoverable patterns and insights."

A Few Suggestions. During a recent demo, I found the Point of Law Results somewhat overwhelming. Maybe it is my "mature" eye issues – but I think my experience of the results would benefit from some color variation or a word cloud to help sort and focus within results.

There is no doubt the legal research is in a state of continuous reinvention. My natural bias is rooted in nested topical hierarchies until I have the "a ha" moment when I finally "get" the benefit of a radically new display. But I have to also admit that Points of Law was not created for me – it was created for the generation of lawyers who grew up clutching a Gameboy and have a natural orientation to digital displays of information.

While Points of Law could be viewed as a response to the Thomson Reuters "granddaddy" of legal headnotes systems, a look at the product evokes similarities to more recent startups: Fastcase (timelines), Ravel Law (citation "constellations") and CARA (explanatory parentheticals). But of course, Bloomberg is adding their own unique twist, rendering, reorganization, reimagining... of an old problem – determining the best authority to support your case and applying AI and Machine Learning to produce a reimagined user experience and workflow.

It is important to note that Bloomberg is still supporting more traditional headnotes and classification systems in their BNA Libraries on Bloomberg Law. It will be interesting to see when and if these classification systems are integrated with the new AI-generated points of law.

The White Paper. To demonstrate the power of Points of Law in conducting case law research on complex, evolving issues, Bloomberg Law developed a new white paper, examining the antitrust law implications of pharmaceutical industry patent disputes. To download the report, visit http://on.bna.com/ywrF3ofoY4t.

Gavelytics: California State Court Analytics Developed by Lawyers for Lawyers

OCTOBER 15, 2017

In law, it seems that frustration is often the mother of invention. Gavelytics is the brainchild of Rick Merrill a former "Big Law" real estate litigator who wanted to get better insights into the rulings and habits of California Superior Court judges. Merrill began developing Gavelytics two years ago when he left Greenberg Traurig. Gavelytics leverages AI, machine learning, and lawyer expertise to deliver their unique brand of California analytics. All I can say is "hallelujah" — someone is finally taking on the challenge of state court analytics.

In a recent interview, Merrill described Gavelytics as being a product "developed by lawyers for lawyers," and designed to address the fact that most lawyers have very little insight into the behavior of state court judges' behavior.

Gavelytics currently covers Los Angeles and Riverside County Superior Courts. They are planning to expand coverage to the 16 most important of California's 58 counties.

I was pleasantly surprised to find this video on their website:

Gavelytics: Determine How Your Judge Will Likely Rule

Figure 37: www.youtube.com/iln1aou1Qk

Features

- *Motion Analyzer* compares each judge's rulings to the overall average rulings of other judges on over 100 motion types.
- *Judicial Workload* – compared to the average judge workload.
- *Gavel Score* – is an indicator of whether a judge tends to rule for plaintiffs or defendants.
- *Sec. 170.6 analyzer.* The California Code of Civil Procedure gives parties the right to make a peremptory motion to disqualify a judge which must be granted. Analytics into how often both plaintiffs and defendants make such motions provides insights into how often and on what types of cases and by which party has each judge been removed in a 170.6 challenge.

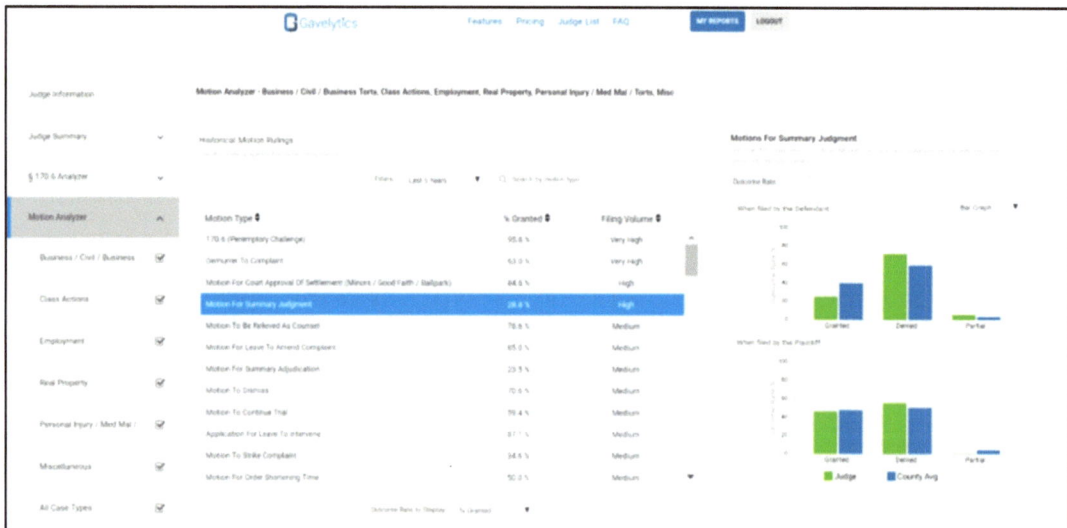

Figure 38: The Gavelytics Dashboard

The Use Cases

Gavelytics can be used for standard analytics use cases including:

- Preparation for a client pitch
- Deciding on filing a peremptory challenge to transfer case to a new judge
- Developing a strategy based on a judge's history
- Managing client expectations regarding timing and outcome.

Future Developments

Merrill indicated that they expect to launch analytics for all 16 of the most important superior courts in northern and southern California by the second quarter of 2018. Longer term, they plan to expand coverage to other states and federal courts. Since they now occupy a unique lead position in state law analytics, I hope they focus on adding products in state courts handling the majority of commercial litigation. New York, New Jersey, Illinois, Texas, and Delaware would be at the top of my list.

Visit the Gavelytics website for more information or to schedule a demo or trial: https://www.gavelytics.com/.

Will a Robot Take My Job? Study Predicts Increased Demand for Lawyers and Librarians Through 2030

OCTOBER 22, 2017

I am an optimist by nature and I have remained skeptical of dark forecasts which predict the future based on one dominant trend (AI comes to mind) while ignoring multiple factors that are likely to moderate or change an expected trajectory. Imagine my surprise and delight to read about a recent study on the future of work which predicted that both lawyers and librarians are two of the careers which are expected to experience increased demand through 2030. "The Future of Skills Employment in 2030" was produced as the result of a collaboration by Pearson – the educational publisher, NESTA – a global innovation foundation, and the Oxford Martin School: (https://futureskills.pearson.com/#/welcome-video).

The report even highlights the surprising inclusion that librarians are listed in the high growth professions: Although traditional libraries have evolved, "We'll still need people: librarians, to help us navigate information both old and new. But like many occupations, the skills profile of a librarian is likely to shift substantially in the years ahead."

The Question Posed: The paper addresses the following research question "Given the likely drivers of change in future labor markets, which occupations would grow or decline in demand by 2030 and what will their skills profile be?

Key trends influencing U.S. and U.K. labor markets include:

- technological change
- globalization
- demographic change
- environmental sustainability
- urbanization
- increasing inequality
- political uncertainty.

Human experts and machine intelligence algorithms analyzed the future of employment and skills. Here are the results:

	UK			USA
1	Food Preparation and Hospitality Trades		1	Preschool, Primary, Secondary, And Special Education School Teachers
2	Teaching and Educational Professionals		2	Animal Care And Service Workers
3	Sports and Fitness Occupations		3	Lawyers, Judges, And Related Workers
4	Natural and Social Science Professionals		4	Postsecondary Teachers
5	Managers and Proprietors in Hospitality and Leisure Services		5	Engineers
6	Health and Social Services Managers and Directors		6	Personal Appearance Workers
7	Artistic, Literary and Media Occupations		7	Social Scientists And Related Workers
8	Public Services and Other Associate Professionals		8	Counselors, Social Workers, And Other Community And Social Service Specialists
9	Other Elementary Services Occupations		9	Librarians, Curators, And Archivists
10	Therapy Professionals		10	Entertainers And Performers, Sports And Related Workers

Figure 39: Jobs in Demand 2030

Frankly I find it surprising that there appears to be so little overlap between the U.S. and U.K. lists of top jobs. Some of this, I assume, can be attributed to the study having used the standard employment categories provided by the U.K. and U.S. governments. Maybe Personal Appearance Workers (6 U.S.) have an equivalence with "Sports and Fitness Occupations" (3 U.K.). But where are the U.K. Lawyers and Librarians? Shall we just blame their disappearance on Richard "The End of Lawyers" Susskind?

Twenty-first century skills that will be in demand in the marketplace in the U.S. include interpersonal skills, teaching social perceptiveness, service orientation, and persuasion. Higher order cognitive skills in demand include: complex problem-solving, originality, fluency of ideas, and active learning.

	UK			USA
1	Judgment and Decision Making		1	Learning Strategies
2	Fluency of Ideas		2	Psychology
3	Active Learning		3	Instructing
4	Learning Strategies		4	Social Perceptiveness
5	Originality		5	Sociology and Anthropology
6	Systems Evaluation		6	Education and Training
7	Deductive Reasoning		7	Coordination
8	Complex Problem Solving		8	Originality
9	Systems Analysis		9	Fluency of Ideas
10	Monitoring		10	Active Learning

Figure 40: Skills in Demand 2030

The report drew six conclusions:

1. Only one in five workers are in an occupation that will shrink.
2. Only one in 10 workers are in occupations that are likely to grow.
3. Seven in 10 workers are in jobs where there is greater uncertainty about the future.
4. Twenty-first century skills will be in demand, but a more nuanced understanding of which skills will be in greatest demand is required.
5. Our research definitively shows that both knowledge and skills will be required for the future economy.
6. Occupations and their skill requirements are not set in stone. Occupations can be redesigned to pair unique human skills of productivity gains from technology to boost demand for jobs.

This will not be a slam dunk. The report provides recommendations that educators, policymakers, and individuals can take to better prepare for a very uncertain future. College degrees may lose some status as other kinds of skills-related credentials emerge which can be acquired throughout the course of a career in order to adapt to emerging demands and opportunities. Jobs will not be set in stone and even the job titles that survive are likely to be radically transformed as they are paired with advances in AI.

Analytics and Insights: It's All About Asking the Right Questions

OCTOBER 31, 2017

Originally printed in: *AALL Spectrum,* Nov/Dec 2017, p.40

Law librarians have been quietly driving the adoption of analytics in business and the practice of law for some time now. They possess the core professional competencies for information assessment that are essential for law firms seeking to leverage analytics for strategic awareness.

Analytics tools enable lawyers to ask completely new questions and gain insights that are virtually unavailable in a text-based research world. Librarians possess the skill set that enables them to ask the right "data quality" questions when firms are assessing the dozens of analytics products competing for a share of lawyers' desktops or an organization's information resource budget. According to the 2017 Gartner Magic Quadrant Report for BI and Analytics Platforms, "By 2020, organizations that offer users access to a curated catalog of internal and external data will realize twice the business value from analytics investments than those that do not."

There is a wide variety of use cases for analytics, including: pitch strategy, alternative fee arrangement responses, litigation strategy, deal negotiation strategy, managing client expectations, driving process efficiency, internal benchmarking, and developing peer metrics.

One pioneering advocate of data analytics in law has been Chicago Kent Law School professor Daniel Katz. When Katz spoke at the July 2017 Private Law Librarians & Information Professionals Summit, his message was clear: "The lawyer of the future will need to be data literate."

Law librarians are also positioned to play an important role in the transformation of legal practice with analytics, because analytics is evolving out of traditional legal research processes and being developed by both traditional legal research providers and innovative startups.

The Challenge of Introducing Analytics

Most lawyers view law as a text-based profession. Professor Katz points out that it is not uncommon for lawyers to dismiss analytics with the comment, "I didn't go to law school to do math." Since lawyers are inherently competitive, the best method of getting them to embrace analytics may be warning them that clients are already embracing analytics to evaluate law firms and litigation strategy. Lawyers who ignore the analytics resources available in their own firm may find themselves confronting the same data presented by a client across the table at a pitch meeting.

The Evolution of Analytics for Litigation and Business Strategy

Over the past five years, there has been an explosion of products and features offering analytics for legal practice insights. These products cover litigation, transactional work, and other specialties, including intellectual property and government affairs work. Many products for litigators are built on the most mundane of data sets: court dockets. However, litigation analytics products have been around for more than a decade. Below are some of the products that have appeared in the last 10 years.

Monitor Suite. Thomson Reuters launched the first interactive legal analytics product in 2005 with the release of Firm 360, which was subsequently rebranded as the Monitor Suite and Intelligence Center. This product was marketed to librarians and competitive intelligence professionals as a stand-alone product for mapping a business development strategy, and it was not offered directly to lawyers on Westlaw. The product offers a robust suite of maps, charts, and competitive data reports that can be used to compare law firms, judges, companies, and industries.

Lex Machina. Lex Machina, which debuted in 2010 as an intellectual property analytics platform, offers the most sophisticated features for interacting, comparing, and filtering results. Lex Machina uses a combination of algorithms, human curation, and tagging to optimize results. Following Lex Machina's acquisition by LexisNexis in 2015, the rollout of new modules has accelerated. Recent modules include securities and commercial and employment law. Lex Machina also offers dozens of standard filters. Each practice module has custom facets and filters to address unique statutory issues, such as damages and remedies related to specific types of litigation. All the modules offer the ability to compare judges, courts, motions, outcomes, remedies, and law firms. Lexis Advance now offers some basic Lex Machina analytics within the research experience.

Bloomberg Law Analytics. In 2016, Bloomberg Law launched their litigation analytics product and became the first major vendor to integrate litigation analytics into an attorney's legal research desktop. Bloomberg leveraged their data on more than 3.5 million companies, 7,000 law firms, and all active federal judges to build their analytics tool. Bloomberg Law analytics is positioned as a strategic planning tool for litigators that offers an analysis of past patterns of judges' behavior, such as motion grants/denials and time to trial. The product also covers all types of litigation in federal courts.

Case Law Insights

Fastcase, Ravel Law, and CARA all use analytics and algorithms to provide unique insights into case law.

Fastcase. Fastcase, which launched in 1999, offers several unique features driven by analytics and algorithms. Fastcase was the first product to offer an interactive timeline that provides a visual litigation history map of an issue in various court systems across a selected time period. Their "forecite" feature recommends cases related to the search that do not specifically match the keywords. The "bad law bot" uses an algorithm to identify and flag negative treatment of a case.

Ravel Law. Ravel Law initially offered a radically reimagined "constellation-like" visualization of case law results. In 2015, they launched Judge Analytics, which used an algorithm to analyze cited cases in a judge's or court's precedential history. The tool offers unique insights for litigation strategy by allowing lawyers to see patterns in how a judge ruled on an issue, and also by highlighting the specific cases and language they use to support a ruling. Ravel Law has subsequently released modules for generating comparative analytics for motions, courts, and law firms.

Casetext. Casetext has offered an open case law system since 2013. In 2016, they launched CARA (Case Analysis Research Assistant). CARA is designed to be used at the end of a drafting process and uses a technique that CARA executives refer to as "brief as query." CARA data-mines the brief by extracting both the text and the citations from the document. The CARA algorithm analyzes direct and "implied" relationships between the cited cases in the brief and related opinions in the Casetext database, and employs latent semantic analysis to sort the results. The CARA results report includes a list of "suggested cases," which are not included in the original brief, and a CARA-generated analysis of those cases. Recently, they have added a feature that analyzes and recommends related law firm briefs.

Can Predictive Analytics Be Far Behind?

Several predictive analytics products are already on the market or getting ready for launch. In 2016, Lexis added a predictive legislation feature to Lexis Advance. The Legislative Outlook Gauge appears with the text of all federal bills and bill-tracking documents. A special Lexis algorithm analyzes historic and current legislative patterns and key probability indicators (e.g., who is the sponsor), to forecast the probable outcome. The algorithms assessment is displayed using an icon that looks like an automobile gas gauge signaling the likelihood of passage.

Manzama, which offers a news monitoring platform to law firms, is working on a predictive platform called Signals. Signals employs data-driven models to inform decision-making by tracking key indicators related to a business or industry that will signal that a trend is forming. Companies and industries will be assigned risk indicators, and Signals subscribers will have a dashboard allowing them to interact with and model the data elements themselves.

The Critical Role of Information Professionals: Asking New Questions About the Data

Although analytics products have some very different qualities than bibliographic resources, the assessment of analytics products involves many of the same fundamental questions of information quality that are second nature to librarians. Librarians are educated to be critics and curators of information resources. Core questions involve the reputation of the source, the provenance of the data, understanding content limitations (dates covered), scope of data (federal vs. state), and the frequency of updating (real-time or delayed). New issues need to be considered, such as whether data elements have been normalized (have law firm and company name variations been corrected?). Are case outcomes classified by keywords or by using semantic analysis? How does the system account for cases with split outcomes such as partial grant, partial denial? What are the assumptions or biases of the algorithm?

Does the vendor offer transparency into the algorithm? These are not easy questions and they are not the only questions. The age of analytics and algorithms is upon us. A new and important role is emerging for information professionals. They will help lawyers ask new questions and gain new insights using analytics. They must demand that vendors clearly define the parameters of the data they are ingesting, analyzing, and displaying in order to help law firms select the best products and gain the best insights for client support and business strategy.

The Future

Analytics are still in their infancy. Products will continue to evolve and improve. Law librarians can have an important impact on encouraging vendors to provide transparency regarding issues related to data and algorithms.

Forget the Robots. You Might Just Need a Clerk. Judicata's Clerk: Algorithms and Analytics that "Grade" and Recommend Edits to Briefs

NOVEMBER 10, 2017

Judicata's Clerk offers so much advanced analysis that it almost scares me. After Judicata founder Itai Gurari, gave me a demo of Clerk I suggested that he needed to put a banner across the top of the screen reminding associates that they still needed to read cases and draw their own conclusions. You load a brief into the platform and Clerk delivers a multi-dimensional critique of the brief supported by a raft of suggestions and analytics.

Gurari has described Clerk as "moneyball for motions." Judicata's Clerk has ingested "thousands of pages of legal text and millions of case data points in order to place each brief in context and provide actionable insights." Different motions have distinct probabilities of being granted in a particular court or by a particular judge. Judicata offers an impressive array of document assessments.

Gurari built Clerk based on the assumption that associates would like to have an easy way to get insight into the strength to weaknesses of their arguments.

Overall   Strong 84

Clerk identified **13 action items** to help improve this brief. Briefs with higher scores have better chances of winning.

	Grade	Score	Action Items
Arguments	Fair	79	6
Drafting	Strong	85	2
Context	Strong	89	5
Overall	Strong	84	13

Have you cited the best cases? Do you have the right ratio of cases supporting your argument and against your arguments? Do any of the cases cited have negative history or have they been granted appeal? Are you misquoting your precedents? These are only a few of the issues that a Clerk report will highlight.

How it Works

Upload a brief into Clerk and it runs an analysis which grades your brief on the following criteria:

- **Arguments:** assess the type, strength, balance and bias of the arguments presented in the brief.
- **Drafting**: Covers the quotation and attribution accuracy of referenced text, and the strength of the briefs supporting precedent.
- **Context**: considers cases with similar causes of action, procedural postures, facts, and judge.

It is impossible to ignore the similarity to the Casetext CARA platform. You upload a brief and in a few seconds, you get results. CARA provides new suggested cases which have not been included in your brief. Judicata delivers a result assessing the quality form and substance in your brief.

Key Facts about Clerk

- Clerk is currently limited to California case law.
- Document types which can be loaded into Clerk are: .doc and text searchable .pdf files.
- Briefs are transmitted using a secure encrypted connection and are not saved, stored, shared, or maintained following the end of a session.

Going Deeper

I can't do justice to the full breadth of Clerk functionality in a blog post. There are eight additional tabs which offer more detailed suggestions on how a brief can be improved. Those tabs are: Briefs, arguments, cases, outcomes, supports, quotations, similar, and judge. Each of these tabs provide suggested action items, insights in the form of an analytic chart and a deep dive into tools and data which will help execute on the "action items" in order to strengthen the brief.

- **Action items** (the what): Action items are the highest priority tasks that Clerk suggests performing.

- **Insights** (the why): Insights provide data and graphs that communicate the context behind Clerk's analysis and Action items.
- **Deep Dive** (the how): Deep Dive provides tools and data to execute on the Action Items, as well investigate further ways to strengthen or attach the brief.

The **Cases** page assists with understanding the citability and precedential value of the cases relied upon in the brief.

Action Items

☑ Add additional support for Garcia v. Joseph Vince Co., which is highly vulnerable to being distinguished.

☑ Add additional support for Dumin v. Owens-Corning Fiberglas Corp., which is highly vulnerable to being distinguished.

☑ Review the five cases to watch listed below to see if they are relevant to this brief.

Figure 41: Action Item suggestions on the Cases Tab

- **The arguments** tab evaluates the arguments presented in the brief and suggest other arguments for consideration.
- **The cases** tab assist with understanding the citability and presidential value of the case is relied upon in the brief.
- **The outcomes** tab identifies outcomes of cases cited within the brief and assists in achieving a good balance.
- **The supports** tab assists with finding the best supporting cases for the legal principles in the brief.
- **The quotations** tab checks the accuracy of quotations to California cases and statutes cited in the brief.
- **The similar** tab provides insight into appeals of decisions involving similar cases including those with the same course of action and posture as the brief.
- **The judges** tab provides context about the judge the brief is filed with and the appeals from their decisions.

Insights

Vulnerability of Cited Cases

Cases that have a high proportion of negative treatments are more vulnerable to being distinguished. Winning briefs tend to rely on fewer vulnerable cases to support their position.

A **significant** number of the cases cited in this brief may be **highly vulnerable** to attack.

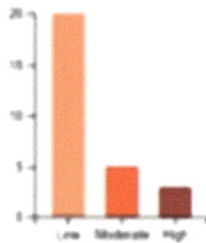

Insights

Outcome Breakdown of Cited Cases

Plaintiffs and defendants both do better when they cite to more cases that go their way. However, the ideal percentage of cases differs by party.

Plaintiffs' briefs do best when citing a roughly 1-to-1 ratio of plaintiff-winning cases to defendant-winning cases. Defendants' briefs do best when citing a 2-to-1 ratio of defendant-winning cases to plaintiff-winning cases.

This brief has a **more than 2-to-1** ratio of defendant-winning to plaintiff-winning cases, which is a **fair** ratio.

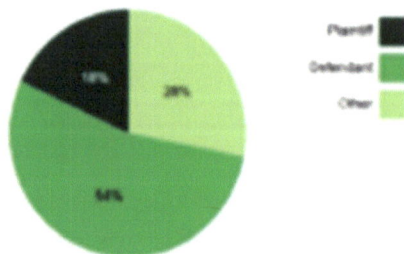

Appealing Party

More plaintiffs appeal from decisions by Judge Peter J. Busch than appeal from
decisions by the average trial court judge, suggesting that Judge Peter J. Busch's
decisions tend to be **defendant-friendly**.

Appeals from Judge Peter J. Busch

Appeals from the average judge

Winning Party

On appeal from decisions by Judge Peter J. Busch, **more defendants win than
average**. Appeals frequently uphold the defendant-friendly decisions by Judge Peter
J. Busch.

Appeals from Judge Peter J. Busch

Appeals from the average judge

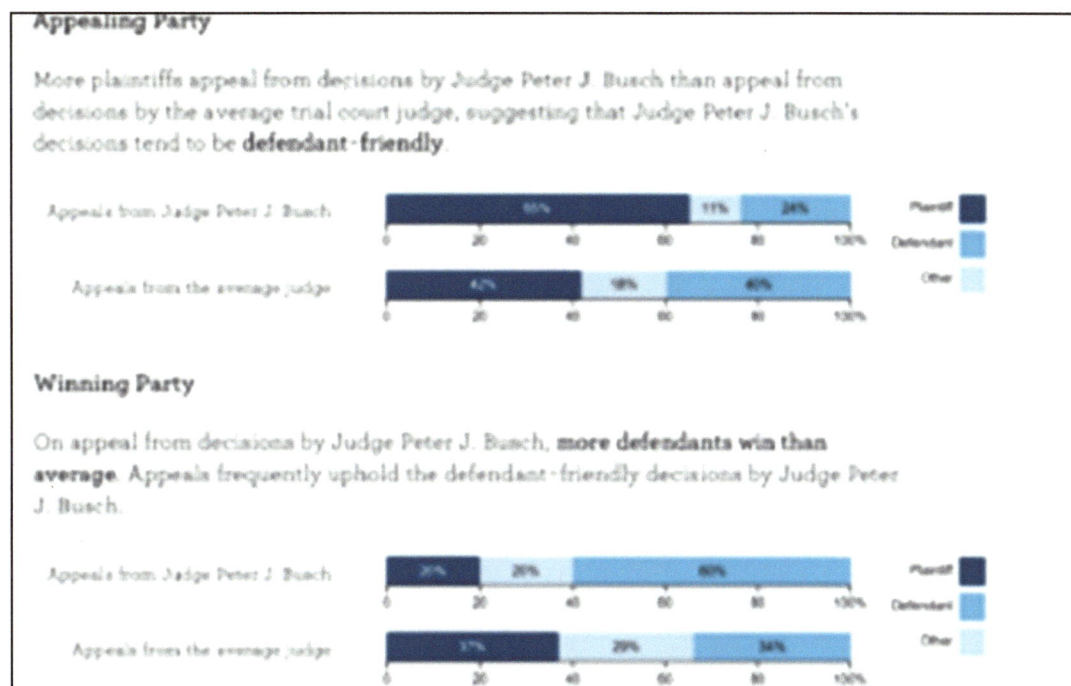

Figure 42: The Judges Tab analytics

The WOW Factor. There is definitely a wow factor to this product. Since I do
not write briefs, I cannot at this point provide a first-hand assessment on whether
I would agree with most or all of the recommendations offered to improve a brief.
Clerk is now being trialed by a number of law firms, and seasoned litigators will
be "kicking the tires" and "checking under the hood" and the ultimate judgment
will be whether the product gets traction in the marketplace.

Clerk leaves the "Robot Lawyer" Products in the Dust. Clerk's approach
to analysis and recommendations is far beyond any other product I have seen
which offers to streamline the litigation drafting process. While Gurari has
avoided the brain numbing hyperbole of AI and robot lawyers in discussing Clerk,
it is clear to me that Clerk delivers more practical insight and workflow efficiency
than any of the wannabe, robot-lawyer products that have been showered with
excessive and uncritical reviews based on what they have promised, rather than
what they can deliver.

Clerk's biggest drawback is that it is exclusively built for California state law.
There are no immediate plans to extend Clerk to federal practice or to other
states. Nonetheless, I am impressed with the Clerk framework and thorough
approach to analysis which uses human and machine intelligence as well as
analytics to help lawyers improve the quality of their work.

It is time for lawyers to move from making decisions based on "anec-data" to making decisions using contextually based analytics. Judicata's Clerk takes a bold step forward and sets a high bar for other legal players who plan to develop drafting products for litigators.

A Clerk demo is available at https://www.judicata.com/demo/clerk.

Lex Machina Releases Products Liability Litigation Analytics Module

NOVEMBER 13, 2017

Today Lex Machina is announcing the release of a new module which covers federal product liability litigation. The Products Liability addition of 500,000 cases pending since 2009 represents the largest expansion of the Lex Machina platform since its launch in 2006.

This data set more than doubles the number of cases which can be analyzed by subscribers.

Products Liability module will provide the same trends in case timing, resolutions, findings, and damages for injuries caused by product defects, including medical devices/pharmaceuticals, vehicles, aircraft, asbestos, and more. It also includes third-party subrogation cases where entities such as insurance companies take over the case on behalf of the plaintiff.

Challenges of Multi-District Litigation. The majority (91%, or 454,166 cases) of federal product liability cases pending since 2009 are part of a multi-district litigation (MDL) – a procedure where cases around the country involving the same incident (or complex set of facts) are transferred and combined into the MDL proceeding for discovery and pretrial. Lex Machina has tagged all of these cases so they can be filtered out of the results in one click. This technique allows researchers to easily compare the data involving only the master case, with the data including all the MDL cases included. Researchers can easily determine whether a presiding judge has expertise with MDL cases, and provides actual judicial rulings about expert witness admissibility.

Products Liability Damages and Findings Tags. According to the press release, Lex Machina interviewed top product liability attorneys to better understand their needs and incorporated their feedback directly into the new offering. As a result, Lex Machina has added 11 new damages tags, including wrongful death/disfigurement, property damage, lost profits, and medical expenses; and 24 new findings, including breach of warranty, defective product, negligence, and consumer protection law violations. Lex Machina's Legal

Analytics is the only platform that incorporates these unique filters into its offering.

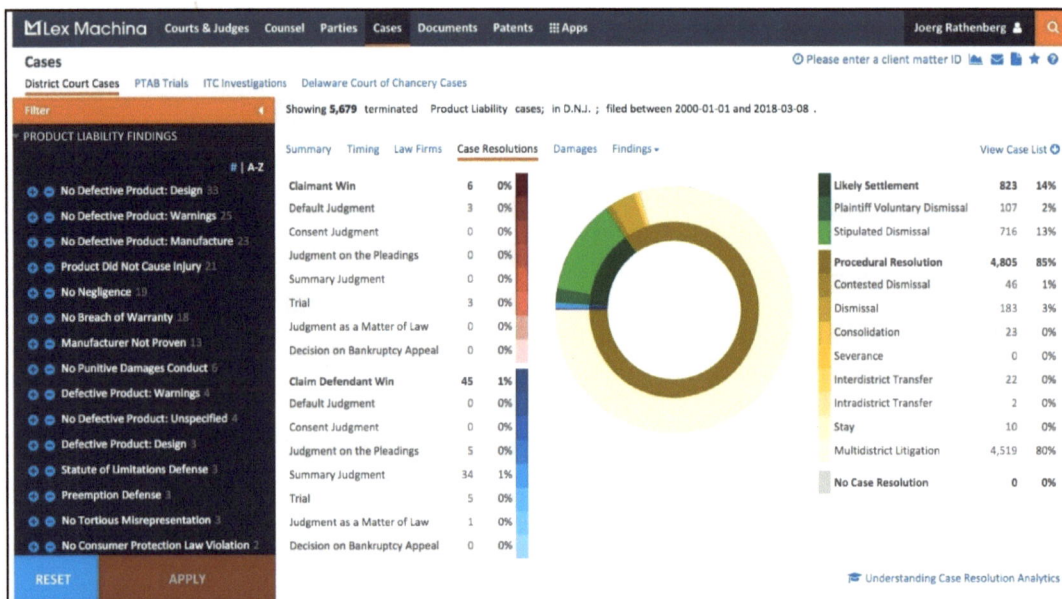

Some of the key product liability insights found within the data include:

- More than 10,300 vehicle-related product liability cases have been pending since 2009. Last year saw the largest number of vehicle-related product liability cases filed (2,226 cases).
- The top three district courts for product liability cases pending since 2009, representing 58% of all filings are: Eastern District of Pennsylvania (29%), Southern District of West Virginia (21%), and Eastern District of Louisiana (8%).
- Asbestos-related filings made up over 140,000 cases pending since 2009 – 97% of which were filed in the Eastern District of Pennsylvania.

CARA Pushes Briefs, Motions, and Analysis of Opposition Documents to Lawyers' Desktops

NOVEMBER 19, 2017

Last May Casetext's CARA launched their "Brief Finder" feature which they recently enhanced with a "push" notification feature. Called "CARA Notifications," it analyzes PACER dockets and delivers an opponent's substantive documents along with a report that highlights missing precedent.

Just to Refresh CARA....

The CARA product uses algorithms and citation analysis to identify relevant case law which is not included in a brief or memo. An attorney can just drag and drop any substantive document into CARA including: (1) an opposing counsel's brief to begin research on your responsive motion and to identify cases not cited by opposing counsel (2) their own draft brief to ensure that the document is not missing relevant authority, and (3) a memo with a legal discussion and case citations to make sure it includes key cases.

"Brief Finder" promises to surface the most relevant legal briefs filed in federal courts by "the country's best law firms." So with no effort, CARA subscribers can see how leading law firms have argued the same issues included in the brief they are drafting.

Waymo LLC v. Uber Technologies, Inc. et al: This will help oppose
RESPONSE to Authorities Cited

Sent Today at 5:16:33 pm (EST)

From Casetext <updates@casetext.com>

Reply-To N/A

BCC N/A

To michellefox@quinnemanuel.com

Subject Waymo LLC v. Uber Technologies, Inc. et al: This will help oppose RESPON
SE to Authorities Cited

casetext

(CARA Matter Update)

Quinn Emanuel Urquhart & Sullivan, LLP subscribes to CARA, an AI-backed
legal research assistant that reviews litigation documents and recommends
relevant case law in seconds. Click below to review CARA's
recommendations, or forward to other members of your litigation team.

CARA RECOMMENDED CASES

RESPONSE to Authorities Cited in *Waymo LLC v.
Uber Technologies, Inc. et al*

11/17/2017 • Northern District of California

1. Veronica Foods Co. v. Ecklin
   Case No. 16 cv 07223 JCS (N.D. Cal. Jun. 29, 2017)

Review Relevant Cases and Holdings

What is CARA NOTIFICATIONS?

Casetext monitors all the PACER dockets in which an attorney has active matters. Whenever opposing counsel files a substantive document such as a brief or memorandum, Casetext retrieves the document, runs it through the CARA analysis algorithm, and delivers the document and a report including uncited but relevant cases to the attorney. Pablo Arredondo, chief legal research, officer believes that "CARA Notifications" is the first legal research product to proactively deliver a custom analysis of an opponent's brief. I have to agree with that assessment. Since excessive research time can be targeted for write-offs, CARA is positioned to target a workflow in need of efficiency drivers.

In a recent interview Amanda Gudis, the head of customer engagement at Casetext, stated that she is getting great feedback from customers about the product. She indicated that partners are especially enthusiastic about the notifications feature because it proactively provides research results which in the past, they would have assigned to an associate and then waited for an answer. According to Gudis there is currently a 35% "click rate" which supports the value of the push notifications. Subscribers receive the documents within an hour of filing. There is no shortage of commercial services which can be set up to monitor PACER filings, but CARA is the only service which delivers only substantive filings and enhances those filings with actionable insights into potential vulnerabilities of those documents. Pablo Arredondo, Casetext's co-founder and chief legal research officer, described how Casetext has applied the same "centrifuge-like" analysis technology that is used in CARA to dockets enabling them to filter out the routine documents and identify only the high value documents.

What's Next for Casetext?

Arredondo was cagey, but he assured me that something exciting is in the works which is currently scheduled to launch January 2018.

AALL Survey Reveals: Budgets, Staffing, Salaries in Law Libraries on the Rise

NOVEMBER 20, 2017

AALL has published its 13th Salary Survey which the AALL Press Release describes as "the only comprehensive, comparative salary information designed by and for legal information professionals at law schools, law firm/corporate law offices, and government law libraries."

In recent weeks there has been a rash of positive stories about the demand for librarians despite the canard that Google had made the jobs of information professionals irrelevant.

Only last week the Wall Street Journal ran a story, "Google Smoogle, Reference Librarians are Busier than Ever," and two weeks ago the educational publisher Pearson released a study predicting an increased demand for librarians through 2030 (https://www.deweybstrategic.com/2017/10/study-predicts-increased-demand-for-lawyers-and-librarians-through-2030.html).

AALL's salary survey confirms that despite the serious disruptions in law firm staffing and the drop in law school enrollments, jobs for information professionals remain steady and are increasing in some environments.

Print vs. electronic

Although all types of libraries: academic, firm, and government have made a dramatic shift from print to digital resources in the past 10 years, the shift has been most dramatic in law firms. The survey also shows that law firms spend, on average, three times more than academic libraries on digital resources.

Table 4: Electronic Information Budget as a Percent of Total Information Budget

		2017	2015	2013	2011	2009	2007
Type of Library	Law School	44%	38%	34%	27%	23%	18%
	Government Law	35%	34%	28%	21%	17%	20%
	Law Firm/Corporate Law	75%	69%	70%	69%	64%	62%

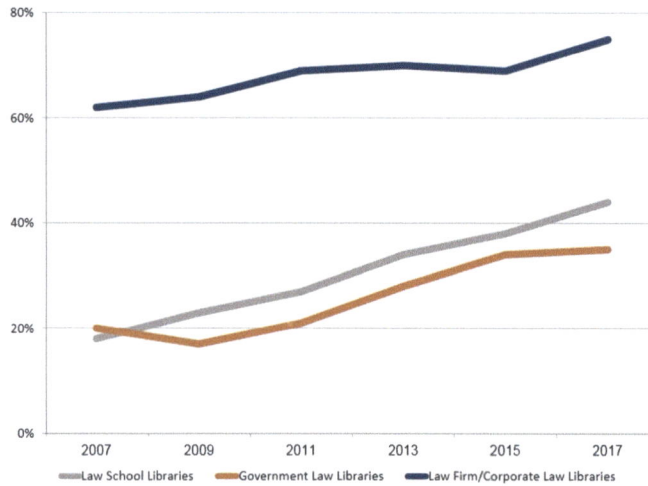

Source: 2017 AALL Salary Survey

Table 3: Hard Copy Information Budget as a Percent of Total Information Budget

		2017	2015	2013	2011	2009	2007
Type of Library	Law School	56%	62%	66%	73%	77%	82%
	Government Law	65%	66%	72%	79%	83%	80%
	Law Firm/Corporate Law	25%	31%	30%	31%	35%	38%

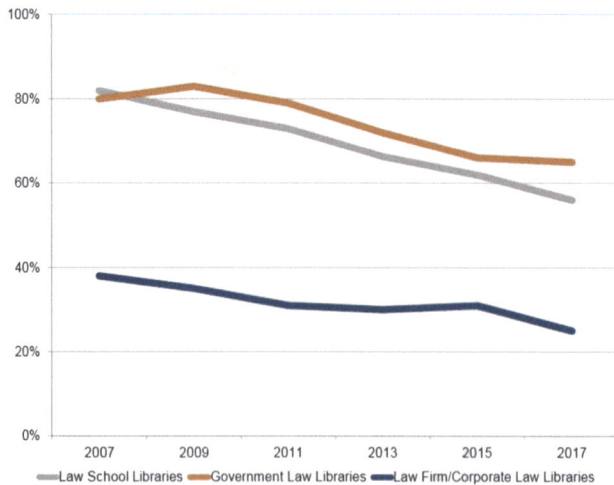

Source: 2017 AALL Salary Survey

What is happening in Law Firms?

Salaries for chief knowledge officers (CKOs) and chief library officers (CLOs) in private law firms jumped 32.1 percent from 2015 to $191,000. The one problem with the survey is that mega-firms are under-represented. While the survey is showing a positive employment and salary trend, it does not include data from the majority for ALM 100 firms. According to the data, only 5 firms with 450+ attorneys responded to the survey. I attribute this low response rate to the structure of the survey which is designed for organization with a single location not for organizations with dozens or even hundreds of locations across the U.S. or around the world.

The data also confirms that law firm librarians are responding to market demands to efficient organizations delivering high value services. An increase in the number of professionals reflects the demand for complex research, competitive intelligence, and knowledge management support. The data shows a decline in paraprofessionals in law firm libraries, reflecting the elimination of low value administrative activities as libraries "climb the value chain," as predicted by Jordan Furlong in his 2013 PLL Summit keynote.

How to Purchase the Survey. The 146-page report in digital format is free for all AALL Members. Non-members can purchase print copies for $250. Information available on the AALL website at https://www.aallnet.org/.

Knowing Value: The Rise of the Law Firm Chief Knowledge Officer

NOVEMBER 28, 2017

Originally published: http://info.legalsolutions.thomsonreuters.com/signup/ newsletters/practice-innovations/2017-oct/article6.aspx

> Knowledge professionals are faced with assessing a complex ecosystem of emerging tools that offer artificial intelligence and analytics. They are on the front line of a workflow-and-intelligence revolution, and bring their experience and expertise to the challenge of marrying external and internal content with algorithms and curated data.

This past July, *The American Lawyer* published its first rebranded annual "Survey of Law Firm Knowledge Management, Library, and Research Professionals." It focused on the rise of the chief knowledge officer (CKO). The main article is titled, "Law Librarian? Try Chief Knowledge Officer." Another article is called, "From Providing Data to Providing Insight." Both articles focused on the emergence of information professionals as CKOs.

Knowledge professionals assess a complex ecosystem of emerging tools that offer artificial intelligence and analytics. The market is full of new products promising law firms "magic bullet" solutions which promise to deliver a competitive advantage, streamlined workflow, or game-changing insights. They are on the front line of a workflow-and-intelligence revolution, and bring their experience and expertise to the challenge of marrying external and internal content with algorithms and curated data. New knowledge and intelligence responsibilities include competitive intelligence, legal project management, lateral partner due diligence, pricing, and pitching, as well as the development of client-facing solutions. Traditional responsibilities include knowledge database management, portal development, and enterprise search.

If law firms expect to thrive in this hyper-competitive legal market, the person responsible for matching products and data to business problems should have a seat at the strategy table. *The American Lawyer* article suggests the obvious conclusion: those firms without a CKO will be at a disadvantage.

Who Becomes a CKO?

CKOs are generally drawn from professionals on two different career paths. Some are law library directors who recognize that the discipline of content assessment, deployment, and management—which they apply to external content—applies to the management of internal content as well. They come to the position with experience in large content-management projects, as well as a deep understanding of lawyers' information-seeking behaviors. Greg Lambert, CKO at Jackson Walker in Houston, Texas, and current President of the American Association of Law Libraries, worked his way up the library ranks from librarian to manager, to director, to CKO. Paul VanderMeer, CKO at Bilzin Sumberg, indicated that he was promoted to CKO when his firm recognized that he had taken on new responsibilities beyond library management, and that the firm's strategy could benefit from a CKO.

Other CKOs are former practicing lawyers who became inspired to pursue a career in knowledge management (KM) from working through the inefficiencies of traditional workflow. Patrick DiDomenico, CKO at Ogletree Deakins and author of Knowledge Management for Lawyers, falls into this camp. DiDomenico, drawing on his personal observations of workflow inefficiencies at regional east coast firm, Gibbons, developed a new job description for himself.

White & Case's CKO, Oz Benamram, describes his calling to KM this way:

> "I was looking for ways to make a bigger impact and have broader influence on how law was practiced. People often get to KM for one of two reasons: to improve accuracy and reduce risk, or to improve efficiency and client satisfaction. I was into making better lawyers, more efficient processes, and providing better client service. The MODEL of practice was more interesting to me than specific lawyering."

Most law firms, if asked if they have an information technology strategy, would not hesitate to say yes. But while knowledge permeates every aspect of the business and practice of law, most firms have not articulated a specific knowledge strategy. Many still engage in stand-alone knowledge projects. DiDomenico points out that the creation of a CKO role demonstrates that a firm is serious about knowledge management, and that the firm is willing to announce that knowledge management is part of their core values and strategy.

How Does a Firm Benefit from an Information Professional in the C-Suite?

CKOs report several important ways that their firms benefit from having information professionals in the C-Suite. Since other key business units also rely on knowledge and analytics from external resources, CKOs see an opportunity to improve the knowledge workflows of their peers engaged in finance, marketing, lateral hiring, client pitches, and pricing. VanderMeer highlighted the opportunity to weave KM tools into new solutions for other administrative departments. One CKO provided this anonymous comment, "We understand the practice management side and can provide a holistic context for projects, attorneys within the firm, peers/competitors in the industry, and clients."

Perhaps most importantly, it is a "win-win." CKOs learn directly from their peers about the challenges each business unit faces. The other Chiefs learn that the firm has a full-time knowledge problem solver with access to resources that can be repurposed for their projects.

Benamram underscores the importance of CKOs:

> "Having a CKO allows firm leadership to engage with someone at a leadership level on important issues related to the development and use of knowledge. It also demonstrates to the entire firm and our clients that we value and invest in knowledge for everyone's benefit. It is not something assumed or taken for granted (or worse, neglected), but rather an important component of the firm. Knowledge as a function can be hard to describe, but with a leader in place it is easier to see that leader in action, what s/he is doing, saying, and therefore to get a better understanding of knowledge as an asset."

The Emergence of Analytics and Algorithms

In the past five years, the legal market has been flooded with pitches from startups offering "game changing" insights derived from public data sources, such as docket-filings and SEC documents. No analytics product can be effectively assessed without a deep understanding of the content behind it. Again, information professionals offer the advantage of having decades of experience assessing these data sets. They know the right questions to ask about quality, data normalization, and other key parameters that determine the true value of any analytics product.

Catherine Monte, CKO at Fox Rothschild, believes that:

> "Analytics tools that ingest, analyze, and report on our own firm's data to provide insights, trends, and opportunities are the ones that will make the most impact. To me this is the heart of what KM is all about: understanding the 'who, what, and why' of a firm and providing insight and solutions. Many of these [products] are integrated with a billing/financial management system so there is a collaborative piece to this and opportunities to team up with other departments. These tools will provide more in-depth understanding of spend, but also metrics, dashboards, and scorecards on other pieces, such as client industry and matter types."

Benamram is seeing the huge impact of algorithms and analytics:

> "Every function of knowledge (research, professional support lawyers, litigation support, and information governance) is either evaluating or has already adopted solutions that incorporate big data analytics and machine learning algorithms. At the moment we have more point solutions in place, but we see the future as having AI-enabled technology as part of our knowledge platforms (e.g., the DMS, enterprise search and content management). I wouldn't say these new technologies are changing our overall approach to collecting and delivering knowledge, but they will help us do it better and faster. Generally speaking, most things that machines can do today, are not things our lawyers or support staff enjoy doing, so automating those functions is welcomed by all."

How Should a Firm Measure the Value of Knowledge Management?

CKOs report that while it is almost impossible to measure the value or return on investment (ROI) for an overall KM strategy, it is possible to measure the benefits of individual projects—if the firm has captured the baseline cost of a process (such as hours spent by various groups of attorneys) before an initiative – and then compare it with the cost in hours after the solution has been implemented.

Bilzen's VanderMeer stated, "While we haven't developed any formal measurements, many, if not all, of our projects are related to improving processes, automating manual processes, or creating data integrations that obviate the need for redundant data entry, all of which are geared towards freeing up lawyer and/or staff time for higher level work."

Clients are clearly indicating that knowledge management initiatives have value to them. They are demanding that firms document their commitment to knowledge management. After becoming CKO at Jackson Walker, pitches and proposals were moved to Lambert's department.

Monte suggested that the best way to determine value "is to have clients or key partners tout the efficiencies, advantages, value, and differentiation of what KM does to their peers or firm management. It's not a hard measurement, but I think this is the most powerful ROI."

What do you think KM Departments will be focused on in five years?

According to VanderMeer, "In five years, I think KM will be squarely focused on leveraging artificial intelligence to improve processes, research, document review, and proofreading, and will allow lawyers to spend less time on routine tasks."

DiDomenico suggests that artificial intelligence and machine learning will have more practical applications, which will reduce repetitive work and allow for the redeployment of attorneys and staff to higher value activities.

Benamram thinks that "KM will be more and more integrated into our lawyers' daily lives, such that it will almost be invisible. They will have knowledge at their fingertips, baked into their practice tools and processes."

It seems clear that even as the tools and methods of KM change over the next five years, the value of knowledge management is on an upward trajectory.

Source

Patrick V. DiDomenico. *Knowledge Management for Lawyers,* Chicago: ABA Book Publishing, 2015.

ALM Legal Compass: Deep Data, Interactive Maps for Legal Market Competitive Insights

DECEMBER 6, 2017

I have to confess that I have a soft spot in my heart for American Lawyer Media. Their flagship publication *The American Lawyer* and I both entered law firms at about the same time. Three decades ago, when the latest issue of *The American Lawyer* arrived, I had the distinct sense that it should have been kept behind the circulation desk and covered in a brown wrapper. By 1980 standards it was a tawdry publication. ALM injected personality, scandal, and ungentlemanly financial comparisons into the rarefied hallways of Wall Street law firms. It had the same "shock factor" as the early postings on the *Above the Law* blog (www.abovethelaw.com). No one wanted to be seen reading it and yet everyone had to take a peek.

In the past 40 years ALM was also a pioneer in the now burgeoning world of law firm analytics. They defined the Profits per Partner metric which for better or worse has become the surrogate for law firm success in the 21st century.

When ALM was repurchased by the Wasserstein investment group in 2014, I worried that the owners might not invest in the ongoing improvement of the ALM platform. The launch of the new *Legal Compass* platform suggests that they recognize there is an insatiable market for competitive insights. *Legal Compass* aggregates the massive archive of Rival Edge data and ALM legal intelligence surveys and married that data with external intelligence mined from dockets, SEC filings, law firm websites, and social media. They have hired data scientists to develop an impressive suite of interactive charts, maps, and data visualization tools.

According to Andrew Neblett, President of ALM Intelligence, "There has been a substantial expansion of data and the product development team to deliver the new platform." It was a massive task to normalize, structure, consolidate, and validate the data from numerous ALM archival data sets and spreadsheets.

ALM has always been an important source of law firm data but frankly their platforms were painfully primitive, inflexible and inevitably frustrating for the user.

The most obvious impact for current subscribers is that two legacy products, *Rival Edge* and *ALM Legal Intelligence* are being phased out and replaced with *Legal Compass*. But Legal Compass offers much more than the sum of those two parts.

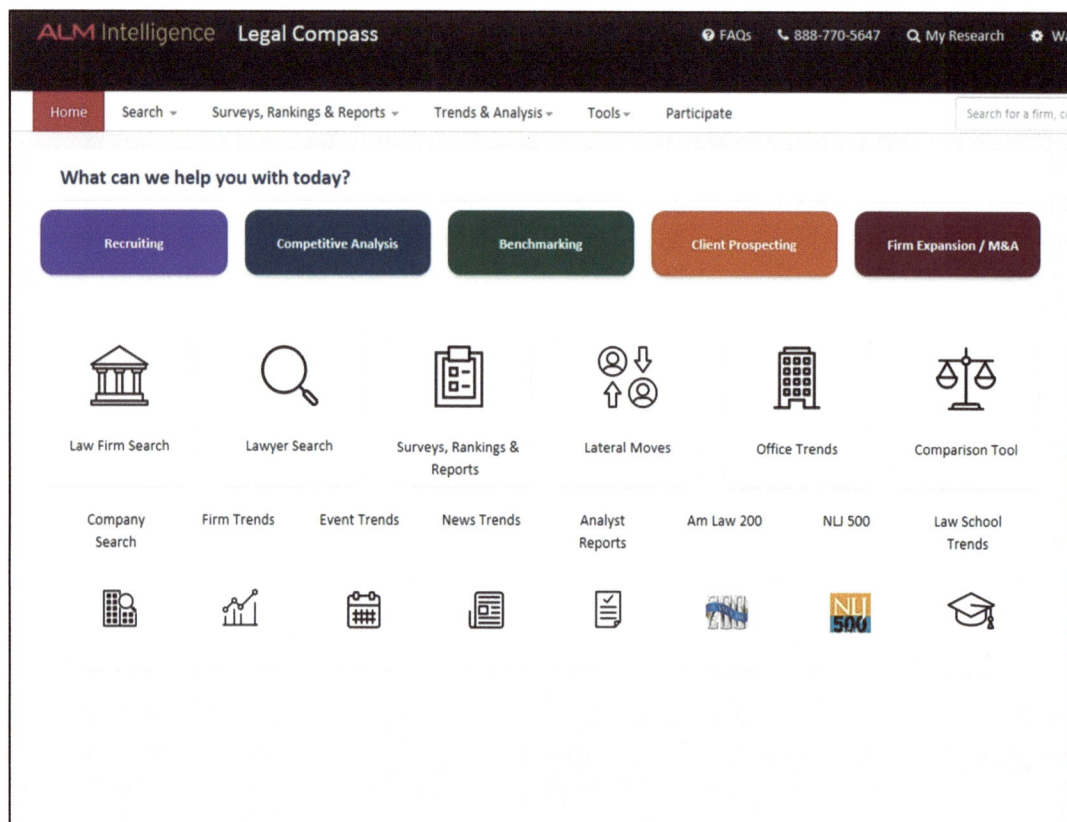

Figure 43: ALM Legal Compass Dashboard

Legal Compass Features

There is no way to describe all the new features and reports available in the Legal Compass platform. The dashboard itself is organized around common tasks: recruiting, competitive analysis, benchmarking, client prospecting, and firm expansion. Research tasks include law firm profiles, lawyer searching, surveys/rankings, lateral moves, office trends, law firm comparisons, company profiles, firm trends, event trends, analyst reports, ALM 200, NLJ 500, and law school trends.

Benchmarking Tools – ALM data forms the backbone of the benchmarking tool which enables firms to compare their own performance against peers and the broader market using unique financial and operational KPIs and a summary of each firm's rankings, practice areas, and financial for the past 10 years. In order to provide context, each firm or group of firms is compared to the overall market using ALM 100 and 200 RPL, PPL data in scatterplot graphs.

Scorecard Charts Scatter Plot	Primary Firm	Comparison Group Median Value	Variance	Primary Firm Trend
Annual Rev. Growth	-2.87 %	1.9 %	-4.8 %	↓
Rev. Per Lawyer	$0.7M	$1.2M	$-0.6M	↓
Cost Per Lawyer	$0.5M	$0.6M	$-0.1M	↓
Profit Margin	26 %	49 %	-23 %	↓
Leverage (Lawyers/Equity Partners)	8.3	3.8	4.55	↑
Profit Per Equity Partner	$1.7M	$3.1M	$-1.4M	↓
Percentage of Equity Partners	32.3 %	58.4 %	-26.1 %	↓
% of Minority Attorneys	17.5 %	18.7 %	-1.2 %	↓
% of Female Attorneys	38.2 %	35.7 %	2.5 %	↑
% of LGBT Attorneys	3.2 %	6.3 %	-3.1 %	↓

Figure 44: Benchmarks Report

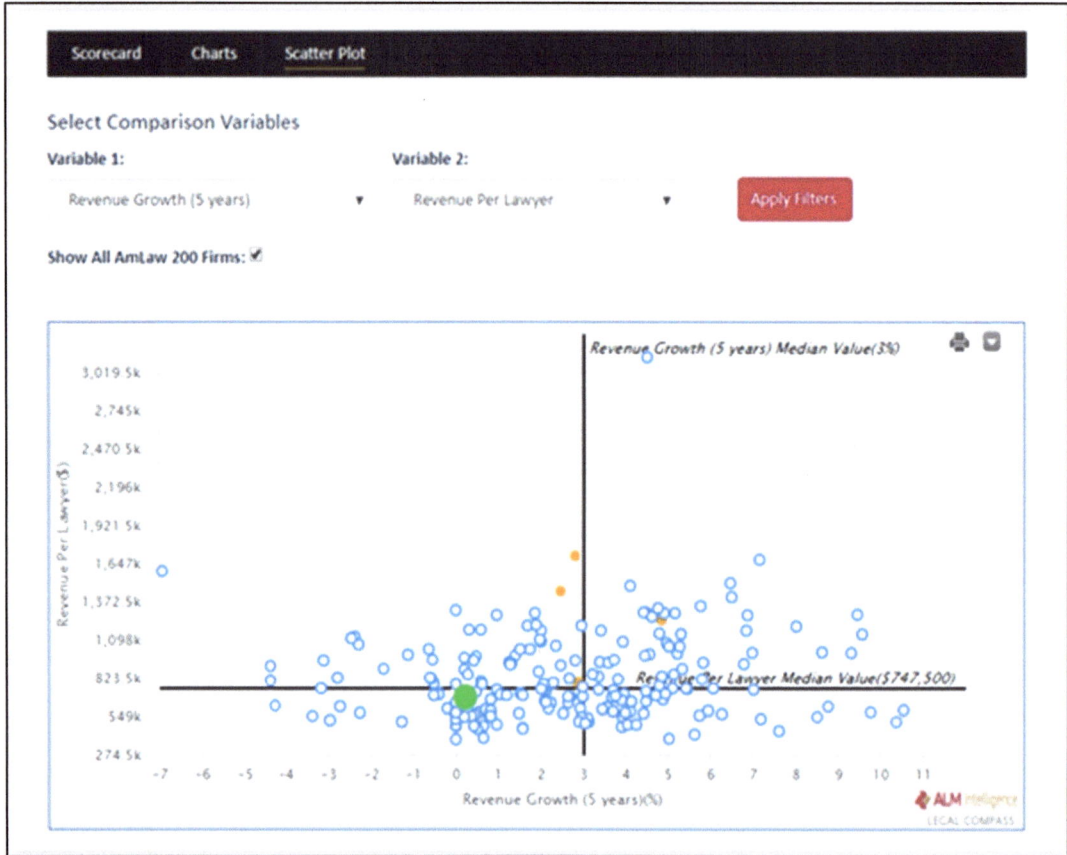

Figure 45: Scatter plot Scorecard

Office Trends Tool– Identify new players and how firms are strengthening or weakening in critical markets and practice areas using interactive maps and charts.

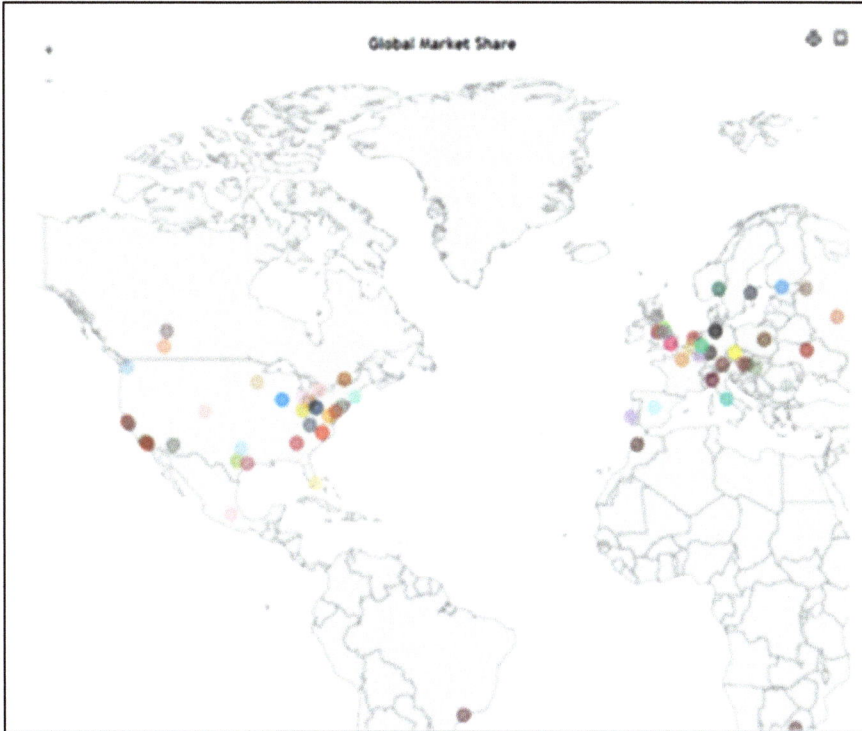

Figure 46: "Office Trends"

Lateral moves tool – reports partner and associate moves by law firm.

	Lateral Hires	#	Lateral Departures	#
Total Moves	All Firms	46	All Firms	240
Top 3 Firms	K&L Gates	3	Greenberg Traurig	4
	Cooley	2	Jones Day	3
	Norton Rose Fulbright	2	Dentons	3
Top 3 Cities	New York	7	London	19
	London	4	New York	17
	Washington	4	Washington	17
Top 3 Practice Areas	Banking and Finance	16	Corporate and Business	116
	Corporate and Business	16	Banking and Finance	108
	Energy, Natural Resources and Environment	8	Litigation	71

Figure 47: Lateral Moves Report

Events and News – Monitors the practice areas and topics competitors are promoting through events, news, and thought leadership.

Diversity Reports – Leverages the archive of diversity data to benchmark against peer firms and the broader industry trends. Since clients are looking more closely at diversity in law firms they have the diversity metrics which they collect from their diversity data. The report offers comparative diversity metrics for each selected firm.

What's Next?

According to Eric Ryles, VP of Customer Solutions, ALM is pursuing a very aggressive development schedule. They plan to release new features every month for the next eight months. These new features will include "law firm intelligence decks" or custom reports and reports on law school graduate career trends. One of the most exciting new modules will be a law firm merger modelling tool which will enable law firm leaders to model a variety of merger scenarios involving specific law firms.

My Two Cents

Since lateral hiring is of increasing importance, yet often proves to be disappointing to both firms and the lateral lawyers themselves, this is an issue in need of new insights. I suggest enhancing the lateral tool with additional metrics to help firms and laterals more accurately predict successful matches. I also suggest enhancing the laterals tool with in-house lawyer moves. Rival Edge has been one of the best but perhaps least known sources of in-house lawyer staffing information. The holy grail would be to expand the company information to include GC organization charts which would associate specific in-house lawyers with specific areas of responsibility e.g. contracting, regulatory, intellectual property, etc.

Practicing Law Institute and Bloomberg Law End Licensing Arrangement

December 13, 2017

Practicing Law Institute (PLI) will be removing their content from Bloomberg Law at the end of 2017 when the current license ends. PLI is one of the premier Continuing Legal Education Providers in the U.S. The big question is: "Will PLI content show up on Lexis or Westlaw?" The answer is "no." According to Craig Miller, the VP of Membership at PLI, the company opted not to continue licensing their treatises and coursebooks to Bloomberg Law or any other third-party publisher in order to focus on developing and promoting their own digital platform, PLI Plus. PLI Plus was previously marketed as PLI Discover Plus. According to Miller, about half of the ALM 100 law firms subscribe to PLI Plus. I have to assume that in making PLI Plus the exclusive platform where researchers can access PLI content, the company is making a play to expand that subscriber list. It was apparent from talking to representatives from both companies that neither intends to burn any bridges.

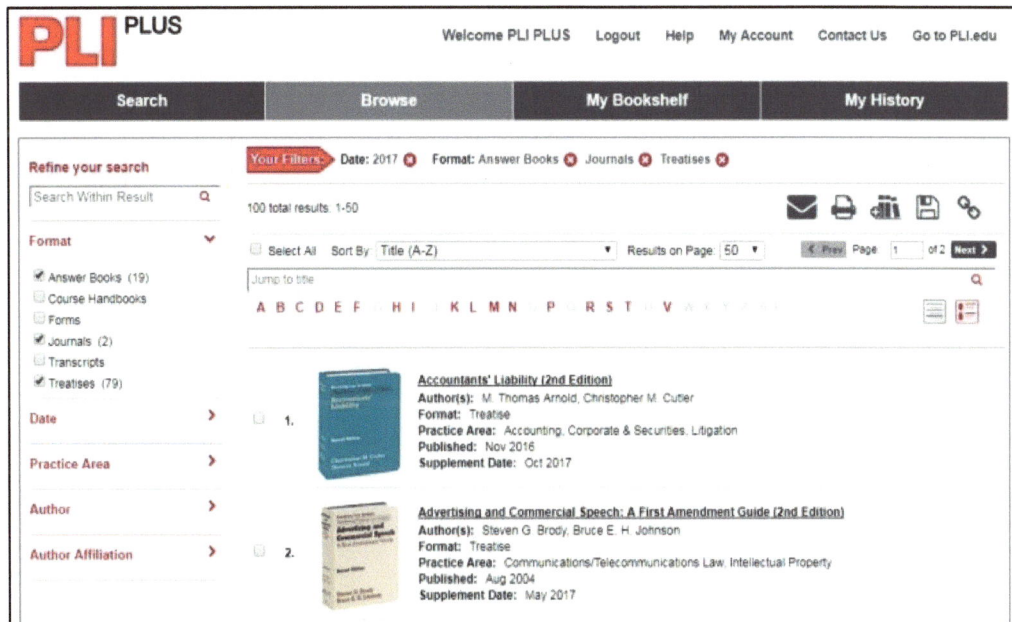

Figure 48: PLI Plus

When Bloomberg Law first launched, it was a platform of primary law materials, which was enhanced with Bloomberg news and financial data. They had very little in the way of legal analysis and commentary. In that context the addition of PLI materials to the platform was a very significant benefit to subscribers. In 2011 Bloomberg acquired the Bureau of National Affairs – a company chockablock with premium editorial legal content. Bloomberg has continued to expand the BNA practice centers and portfolio series and Practical Guidance Suites, while also adding treatises from third party publishers such as the Federal Judicial Center.

PLI Plus includes an archive of PLI treatises, coursebooks, answer books, legal forms, and program transcripts. The PLI Plus website includes 90,000 legal research documents covering 25 practice areas.

PLI Needs Primary Law: What About a Mashup with Fastcase or Casetext? A Win-Win Scenario?

The PLI content on Bloomberg was enhanced with links to primary sources such as cases and statutes. Hyperlinking is a common feature in most legal research platforms. PLI could benefit from a relationship with lower cost legal research providers such as Casetext and Fastcase. Fastcase has already entered into several alliances with outside content providers most notably HeinOnline. Either Fastcase or Casetext could benefit from the addition of PLI materials, which include both treatises and workflow materials such as checklists and forms. While PLI had indicated that they want to be the exclusive provider of their own content, this would not rule out their licensing content from another vendor which will enhance their user experience.

Bloomberg Law Adds Judges Analytics, New York Commercial Practice Portfolio, and Docket Key for Searching Within Dockets

DECEMBER 17, 2017

Bloomberg Law recently announced three enhancements to Bloomberg Law which will be available to all subscribers at no additional cost. These resources include "time to trial" analytics, a unique court focused practice portfolio, and a groundbreaking new docket feature, Docket Key, which will bring a smile to the face of anyone who has ever spent hours slogging through a docket sheet trying to find a specific document.

Analytics for Time to Motion Grant and Case Resolution

The new analytics feature allows lawyers to analyze judges on time to motion grant or resolution by case type. Judges and district court case timing can be compared to each other and to the average overall case timing. As clients become more price sensitive, predictive analytics on case and motion timing can be used for both pitches and early case assessment.

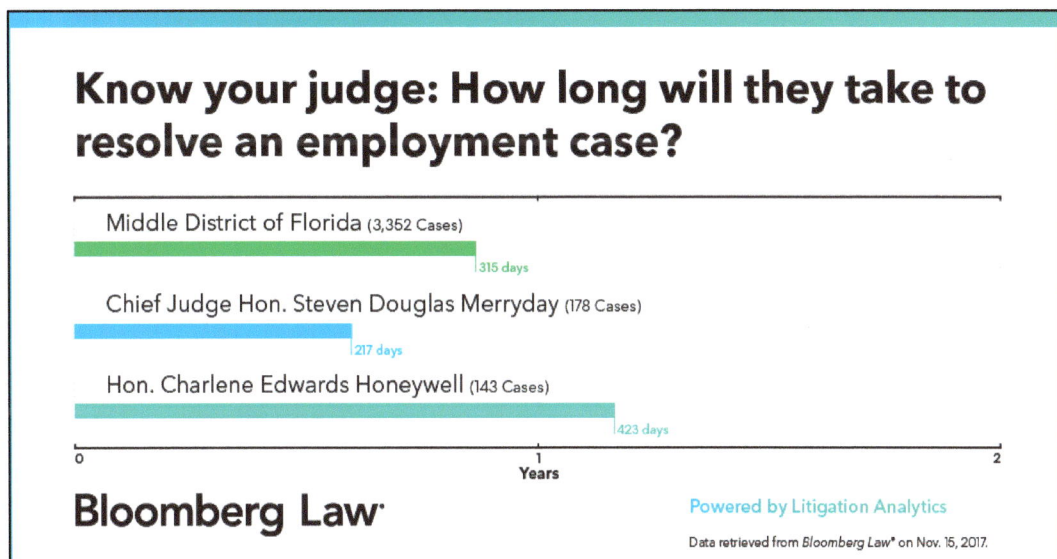

Know your judge: How long will they take to resolve an employment case?

Middle District of Florida (3,352 Cases)
315 days

Chief Judge Hon. Steven Douglas Merryday (178 Cases)
217 days

Hon. Charlene Edwards Honeywell (143 Cases)
423 days

0   1 Years   2

Bloomberg Law

Powered by Litigation Analytics

Data retrieved from *Bloomberg Law* on Nov. 15, 2017.

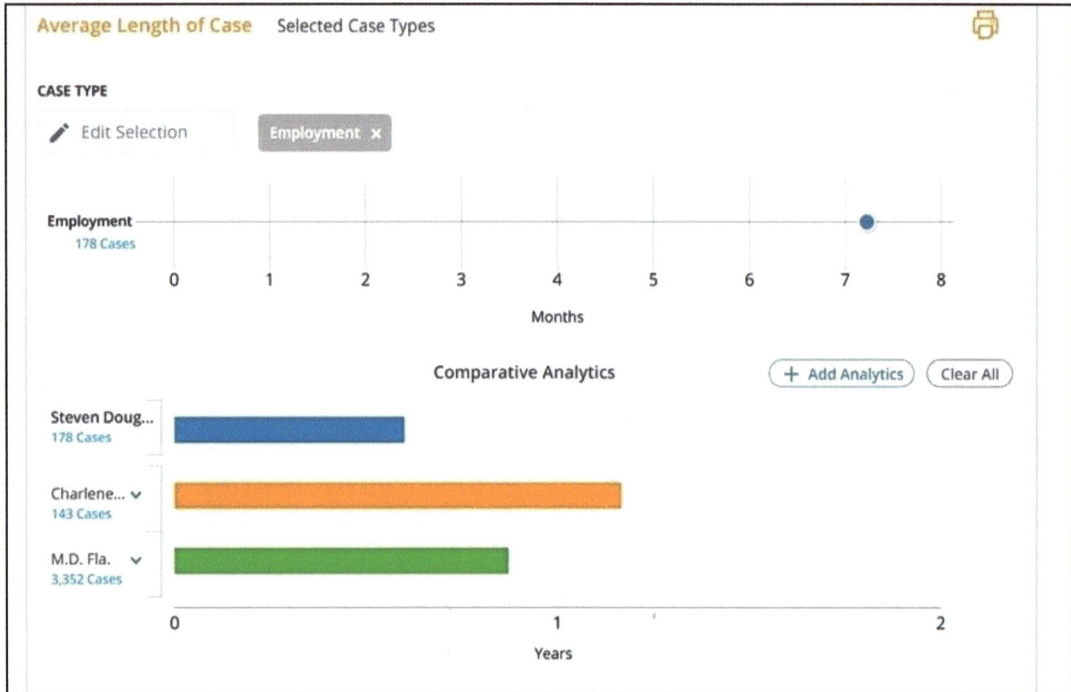

Figure 49: Analytics comparing judges and district time to trial.

NY Commercial Division Practice – Bloomberg Law has partnered with the law firm Patterson Belknap to create a new civil practice guide which focuses on commercial litigation in the Commercial Division of the New York Supreme Court. Unlike every other state, in New York the Supreme Court is in fact the trial court – not an appellate court. Bloomberg has intensified their focus on developing practice resources that can enhance efficiency and workflow. They now have 13 sets of practice portfolios. I have previously pointed out that BNA's practice portfolios were print resources which focused on streamlining workflow, and they predated Practical Law by several decades. They had the misfortune of being developed in the "bad old days" when offering lawyers tools to drive efficiency was met with a laugh or a yawn.

According to the press release, the commercial division of the New York State Supreme Court was "formed to enhance the quality of judicial adjudication and improve efficiency of commercial disputes. The commercial division practice presents unique challenges because lawyers need to understand both the state rules of procedure as well as the specific rules of the commercial division." The portfolio provides insight into the inner workings of a commercial division and covers issues including the selection of judges, the rules of practice jurisdiction, management of cases, and discovery motion practice, as well as appeals from the court.

Docket Key (Hooray! Finally, a Way to Search for Specific Documents)

Anyone who does docket research knows that dockets are loaded with cryptic entries which do little to identify the exact nature of the documents associated with each entry. Docket Key is one of the first attempts by any publisher to take a stab at solving this problem. Docket Key makes locating specific filings easy. Bloomberg employed machine learning to identify 20 categories of documents including motions, complaints, notices briefs, and orders.

Currently Docket Key supports the most frequently searched 15 federal districts on Bloomberg Law including the Southern District of New York, the Eastern District of New York, the District Court of the District of Columbia, and the Northern District of California. Docket Key is a search feature on the docket search page and enables researchers to navigate directly to a desired document. For a relative newcomer to the legal research arena, Bloomberg has always had an exceptionally strong docket product. Lexis and Westlaw have had docket products on the market for decades, so it is a real "head scratcher" that they have let Bloomberg leapfrog over them in streamlining docket research and making specific document types discoverable within a docket sheet. It doesn't sound like rocket science – but Bloomberg is the first one to get "lift off" on this particular challenge.

Users will notice that Bloomberg has already replaced their recently revised Dockets page. This new version eliminates tabs and reduces the number of clicks to get to a result.

Index

Products Reviewed in 2017

Wolters Kluwer

About the Author

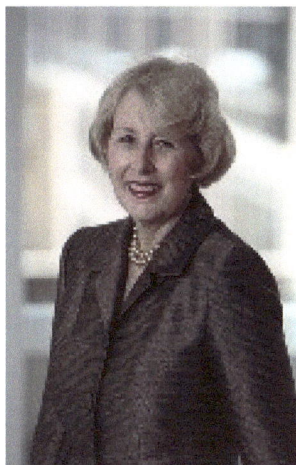

Jean P. O'Grady is currently Sr. Director of Information, Research & Knowledge at DLA Piper US, LLP. She has over 30 years of experience developing strategic information initiatives for Amlaw 100 law firms. She holds a J.D. from Fordham University School of Law, an M.L.S. from St. John's University and a B.A. in History from Fordham University She is a member of the NY State Bar. She has previously held Director positions at WilmerHale in DC and Shea & Gould in NY. She began her career as a reference librarian at the Pace University School of Law. She has been an adjunct faculty member at the graduate schools of Library and Information Science at St. John's University and Long Island University where she taught legal research courses.

Professional Activities: Chair of the Private Law Libraries Section of the American Association of Law Libraries (2013-2014) and a past President of the Law Library Association of Greater New York (1991-1992); Board Member of the American Association of Law Libraries (2017-2019); Board Member, New York Law Institute (2015-2018).

O'Grady is a frequent author and speaker on the transformation of libraries and information centers, digital contract licensing, knowledge management, legal analytics and the legal publishing industry. She has spoken at programs sponsored by the Information Industry Association, the Association of Newsletter Publishers, Practicing Law Institute, International Legal Technology Association, West Publishing, Price Waterhouse, LegalTech, Lexis-Nexis. Janders Dean Knowledge Management Conference, American Association of Law Schools, as well as the American Association of Law Libraries, Canadian Association of Law Libraries, Australian Law Libraries Association, and the Special Libraries Association.

In 2011 she launched "Dewey B Strategic" to promote awareness of the strategic importance of librarians, libraries, and knowledge managers as change agents and innovators in the organizations they support. She has written provocative pieces on a variety of law firm management, publishing, and technology issues which have sparked important debates in the industry.

Honors Include:

2011: Named to the FastCase 50 top legal innovators.

2013: Elected to the Board of Directors of the New York Law Institute.

2104: Inducted as a Fellow in the College of Law Practice Management. Fellows of the College are distinguished law practice management professionals who represent law firms, educational institutions, professional associations, and other organizations that contribute to excellence in law practice management.

2015: Co-Chair of the ABA, Law Practice Management, Knowledge Strategy Committee.

2016: Named an ABA Magazine "Legal Rebel."

2016: AALL Presidential Certificate of Appreciation.

2017-2019: Elected Board Member, American Association of Law Libraries.

"Dewey B Strategic" named to the ABA Magazine Blawg 100 in 2012, 2013, 2014, 2015. 2016. Inducted in the Blawg 100 Hall of Fame 2016.

www.ingramcontent.com/pod-product-compliance
Lightning Source LLC
Chambersburg PA
CBHW041453210326
41599CB00005B/234